SQL Crash Course for Beginners

A Thrilling Challenge to SQL Mastery

Mark Reed & CyberEdge Press

© Copyright 2024 - All rights reserved.

The content contained within this book may not be reproduced, duplicated or transmitted without direct written permission from the author or the publisher.

Under no circumstances will any blame or legal responsibility be held against the publisher, or author, for any damages, reparation, or monetary loss due to the information contained within this book, either directly or indirectly.

Legal Notice:

This book is copyright protected. It is only for personal use. You cannot amend, distribute, sell, use, quote or paraphrase any part, or the content within this book, without the consent of the author or publisher.

Disclaimer Notice:

Please note the information contained within this document is for educational and entertainment purposes only. All effort has been executed to present accurate, up to date, reliable, complete information. No warranties of any kind are declared or implied. Readers acknowledge that the author is not engaged in the rendering of legal, financial, medical or professional advice. The content within this book has been derived from various sources. Please consult a licensed professional before attempting any techniques outlined in this book.

By reading this document, the reader agrees that under no circumstances is the author responsible for any losses, direct or indirect, that are incurred as a result of the use of the information contained within this document, including, but not limited to, errors, omissions, or inaccuracies.

Table of Contents

INTRODUCTION xi

CHAPTER 1: Introduction to SQLia 1

    What Are Databases? 1

        Relational Databases (SQL) 2

        Non-Relational Databases (NoSQL) 2

    Why Databases Matter 2

        Real-Life Analogy 3

    Exploring SQLia's Kingdoms—Relational vs. Non-Relational Databases 3

        The Relational Kingdom (SQL) 3

        The Non-Relational Realm (NoSQL) 4

    Your First Spell—Casting SELECT and FROM 4

    Navigating the Libraries—The Power of FROM 5

    Real-Life Scenarios—How Databases Shape SQLia and Beyond 5

        E-Commerce 6

        Social Media 6

    The Mystical Power of WHERE 6

    Sorting the Scrolls—ORDER BY 6

    Final Challenge—Can You Defeat the Data Dragon? 7

    Conclusion: The Journey Continues 7

CHAPTER 2: Exploring the Fields of Data 9

    Understanding Tables and Their Structures: Laying the Foundation 9

        The Layout of the Treasure Map 10

    Primary Keys: The Rulers of Uniqueness 10

        Why Primary Keys Matter for Your Quest 10

    Foreign Keys: Building Alliances Between Kingdoms 11

        The Role of Foreign Keys in Your Data Empire 11

    The Secret Art of Normalization: Keeping Your Data Pristine 12

    Introduction to Columns and Data Types: The Tools of Your Trade 12

Guarding Your Data with Constraints: The Royal Guard of Your Database 13
   The Most Trusted Guards 13
Mastering the SELECT Spell: Querying Specific Columns 14
Using Aliases: Nicknames for Your Columns and Tables 14
Designing Efficient Tables: Building the Kingdom's Infrastructure 15
   Guidelines for a Robust SQL Castle 15
Boss: The Guardian of Data Integrity 16
   Boss Overview 16
   Phase 1: Unique Integrity 16
   Phase 2: Relational Integrity 17
   Phase 3: Domain Integrity 18
   Phase 4: Referential Integrity 19
   Victory! 19

CHAPTER 3: The Quest for Precision—Filtering Data 21
The Sword of Precision: The WHERE Clause 21
   The Importance of the WHERE Clause 22
   Understanding the Syntax Structure of WHERE Clauses 22
Practical Application Examples: Wielding the Sword 23
Avoiding Pitfalls: The Dangers of Filtering 24
   Case Sensitivity 24
   Logical Operator Misuse 24
   Performance Issues 24
The Arcane Power of Comparison Operators 24
   Equals (=) 24
   Not Equal (<>) 25
   Greater Than (>) and Less Than (<) 25
Combining Conditions With AND and OR: A Balancing Act 25
Common Pitfalls in Combining Conditions 26
Hands-On Practice: Sharpening Your Skills 27
Final Thoughts: Becoming the Master of Data Filtering 27

    Boss: Conquering Complex Filtering 28

        The Boss's Challenge: The Kingdom of TradeMaster 28

        Conquering the Challenge: Crafting the Ultimate SQL Queries...............................29

        Victory: Defeating the Final Boss 31

CHAPTER 4: Aggregating Adventures—Summarizing Data 32

    The Power of Aggregate Functions: Your Trusted Tools 32

        The COUNT Function: Your Treasure Map 33

        The SUM Function: Gathering Gold Coins 33

        The AVG Function: Finding Balance 34

        MIN and MAX: The Scouts of Extremes...35

    Grouping Your Findings: The Art of ORDER and HAVING 36

        GROUP BY: Organizing Your Loot 36

        HAVING: Refining Your Search for Treasure 37

    The Final Boss: The Maze of Complex Queries 37

    Handling NULL Values: The Phantom Data...38

        Conclusion: A Master of SQLia 39

CHAPTER 5: Joining Forces—Combining Tables 40

    INNER JOIN: The Hero of Table Joins...40

        Basic Syntax of INNER JOIN 41

        Real-World Examples of INNER JOIN 41

        Visualizing INNER JOIN 42

        INNER JOIN for Advanced Data Insights 42

    LEFT JOIN and RIGHT JOIN: The Dynamic Duo 42

        LEFT JOIN...42

        RIGHT JOIN 43

        Practical Use Cases of LEFT and RIGHT JOIN 43

        When to Use LEFT JOIN or RIGHT JOIN 44

    FULL OUTER JOIN: The Best of Both Worlds 44

        Basic Syntax of FULL OUTER JOIN..44

        Practical Example of FULL OUTER JOIN..44

CROSS JOIN: Exploring Every Possibility 45
Basic Syntax of CROSS JOIN 45
Practical Example of CROSS JOIN 45
Combining Joins: The Multi-Join Mastery 45
Practical Applications of SQL Joins in Various Industries 46
Business Analytics 46
Healthcare 46
Boss: The Grandmaster of Joins Challenge 47
The Scenario: The Ultimate E-Commerce Data Quest 47
Step 1: The Customer Orders Report 48
Step 2: Identifying Unshipped Top Products 48
Step 3: Department Sales Analysis 49
Bonus Round: Advanced Querying With Multiple Joins 50
Victory! 51

CHAPTER 6: Unveiling the Hidden—Subqueries 52
Defining Subqueries: A Key to Unlock Complex Solutions 52
Subqueries vs. Joins: Picking Your Weapon 53
How to Write Subqueries: Following the Map 54
The Secret Power of Subqueries 54
Correlated Subqueries: The Real-Time Oracle 55
Non-Correlated Subqueries: The Silent Companion 55
Advanced Techniques: EXISTS, ANY, and ALL 56
EXISTS Subqueries 56
ANY and ALL 56
Practical Challenges: Gearing Up for Real-World Quests 57
Challenge 1: Employee Performance 57
Challenge 2: Inventory and Restocks 58
Challenge 3: Customer Loyalty 58
Advanced Performance Optimization for Subqueries 58
Indexing for Faster Subqueries 59

    Converting Correlated Subqueries to Joins 59

    Temporary Tables and Common Table Expressions (CTEs) 60

  Boss Battle: Complex Subqueries 60

    Final Challenge: Department Performance Review 60

    Final Thoughts: Becoming a Subquery Master 61

CHAPTER 7: Data Wizards—Functions and Expressions 62

  String Functions: CONCAT, LENGHT, SUBSTR 62

    CONCAT: Combining Strings for Enhanced Data Output 63

    LENGTH: Ensuring Data Integrity through String Length Validation 64

    SUBSTR: Extracting the Most Relevant Data 65

  Date Functions: NOW, DATE_ADD, DATEDIFF 66

    NOW: Capturing the Present Moment 66

    DATE_ADD: Projecting into the Future 66

    DATEDIFF: Measuring Durations and Time Gaps 67

    Combining Date Functions: A Holistic Example 68

  Real-World Use Cases of Date Functions 68

  Mathematical Functions: ABS, ROUND, POWER 70

    ABS: Handling Negative Numbers and Variances 70

    ROUND: Ensuring Precision in Financial and Statistical Reporting 71

    POWER: Empowering Advanced Calculations and Forecasts 72

    Practical Applications of Mathematical Functions 73

  Conclusion 73

CHAPTER 8: Conquering the Chaos—Advanced Joins and Set Operations 75

  Cross Joins and Cartesian Products 75

    Mission: The Endless Pairing 76

    Bonus Challenge: The Optimized Pairing 76

  The Duel of UNION vs. UNION ALL 77

    Mission: Unite the Divided Kingdoms 77

    Bonus Challenge: Preserve Every Record 77

    Strategy Tip: When to Use UNION vs. UNION ALL 78

- The Bridge of INTERSECT ... 78
  - Mission: Find the Common Warriors ... 78
  - Bonus Challenge: Discover the Common Treasures ... 78
  - Advanced Challenge: Finding Common Ground Across Multiple Tables ... 79
- The Trial of EXCEPT ... 79
  - Mission: Find the Unique Warriors ... 79
  - Bonus Challenge: Reveal the Untouched Lands ... 79
  - Advanced Challenge: Identifying Non-Customers ... 80
- Boss: The Data Kraken ... 80
  - Mission: Untangle the Kraken's Chaos ... 81
  - Step 1: The Tentacles of Chaos – Cross Joins Everywhere ... 81
  - Step 2: The Duplicates Surge – UNION vs. UNION ALL ... 81
  - Step 3: The Grip of Commonality – INTERSECT Challenge ... 82
  - Step 4: The Kraken's Final Weakness—EXCEPT Operation ... 82
  - The Final Blow: Synthesize the Data ... 83
  - Victory: The Data Kraken Falls ... 83

CHAPTER 9: Building Strongholds—Views and Indexes ... 85
- Crafting Your Data Fortress—Views ... 85
  - Constructing a View—Simplify Your Data ... 85
  - The Power to Alter or Destroy Views ... 86
  - Integrating Views Into SQL Queries ... 87
- Fortifying Your Stronghold—Indexes ... 88
  - Understanding Index Basics ... 88
  - Different Types of Indexes—Choose Your Arsenal ... 88
  - Striking a Balance—Read vs. Write Performance ... 89
- Advanced Indexing Tactics—Optimizing Your Stronghold ... 90
  - Partial Indexes—Focusing Your Defense ... 90
  - Indexed Computed Columns—Efficiency Meets Power ... 90
  - Monitoring and Tuning Your Database Stronghold ... 91
- Boss: The Fortress Keeper Challenge ... 92

    Boss Battle Quest: The Ultimate Performance Test 92

    Step 1: Create the Ultimate View 92

    Step 2: Power Up with Indexes 93

    Step 3: Analyze with EXPLAIN 93

    Victory: Conquering the Fortress Keeper! 93

CHAPTER 10: Guardians of Data—Transactions and Security 95

    The Art of COMMIT and ROLLBACK 95

        Understanding Transactions 95

        Using COMMIT: Claim the Treasure! 96

    The Battle of Concurrent Transactions 98

        Isolation Levels: Choosing Your Shield 98

        Using Isolation Levels: Preventing Transaction Collisions 98

        Locking Mechanisms: Securing the Gates 99

        Locking Down the Vault: Exclusive Locks in Action 99

    User Privileges—Controlling Access 100

        Granting Privileges: Assigning Roles to Trusted Allies 100

        Revoking Privileges: Cutting Off Access 101

    Role-Based Access Control (RBAC)—Building a Secure Hierarchy 101

        Creating Roles: Empowering the Kingdom 101

    Boss Battle: The Final Trial—The Siege of Data Integrity 102

        Stage 1: Transactional Turmoil—The Flood of Uncommitted Changes 102

        Stage 2: The Lockdown—Breaking Through the Fortified Gates 103

        Stage 3: The Invasion of Intruders—Unauthorized Access 104

        Final Victory: Defeating the Chaos Bringer 105

CHAPTER 11: The Final Boss Battle: Real-World Scenarios 107

    Entering the Arena: Identifying Customer Trends—The Crystal Ball Quest 107

        Challenge #1 108

        Challenge #2 108

    Monitoring Sales Performance—The Scorekeeper's Challenge 109

        Challenge #3 109

    Challenge #4 110
  Resource Allocation—Mastering the Art of Efficiency 110
    Challenge #5 110
    Challenge #6 111
  Generating Reports—The Scribe's Dilemma 111
    Challenge #7 112
    Challenge #8 112
  Debugging and Optimizing Queries—The Code Whisperer's Challenge 113
    Challenge #9 113
  Final Boss Battle: Defeating the Data Demon 114
    Phase 1: The Resource Allocation Challenge 114
    Challenge #1: Identifying Stock Shortages 114
    Challenge #2: Optimizing Staffing Levels During Peak Hours 115
    Phase 2: The Performance Optimization Gauntlet 115
    Challenge #3: Improving Query Performance 116
    Challenge #4: Implementing Indexing for Speed Boosts 116
    Phase 3: The Report Generating Showdown 117
    Challenge #5: Sales Performance by Region 117
    Challenge #6: Custom Report for Stakeholders 118
    Final Strike: The Data Demon Defeated 118
Conclusion 120
References 124

Introduction

You're stepping into a vibrant realm where every line of code unlocks new treasures, and every challenge transforms you into a powerful data wizard. Welcome to SQLia—where your adventure into the magical world of SQL begins! Picture yourself as the hero of this grand story, armed not with swords or spells but with knowledge and curiosity. Your journey will be filled with intriguing puzzles, unexpected allies, and formidable foes, all set against the backdrop of the mysterious and fascinating universe of SQL. This is no ordinary learning experience; this is an epic quest where each command you learn is a step closer to mastering the vast landscape of data that powers our world.

In today's digital age, data is everywhere—it's the invisible force shaping decisions, guiding innovations, and driving progress. From the apps we use daily to the massive networks that connect us globally, data is the lifeblood of the modern world. Think of it as the pulse of businesses, governments, and institutions. Without it, decision-making would be reduced to guesswork, a shot in the dark. And this is where SQL—Structured Query Language—becomes your trusty map and compass, guiding you through the vast oceans of information, and helping you extract meaning and insights. Learning SQL isn't just an academic exercise; it's a transformative skill that empowers you to harness the full potential of data. Whether you're aiming to boost your career, tackle complex projects, or simply satisfy your intellectual curiosity, SQL is your gateway to endless possibilities.

Imagine walking into a bustling marketplace—vibrant stalls overflowing with fresh produce, colorful fabrics, and exotic spices from far-off lands. Now, instead of merchants, each stall is filled with datasets brimming with hidden stories, insights, and secrets just waiting to be uncovered. SQL is your key to unlocking these treasures. With it, you can sift through piles of seemingly random numbers and text, pulling out patterns, uncovering trends, and finding truths that can transform otherwise mundane data into powerful narratives. It's like being a detective, piecing together clues to solve a grand mystery, except your clues are hidden in rows and columns of data, and your tool is the SQL query.

But why stop at simply understanding data? This journey through SQLia is designed to be more than just a technical manual—it's an adventure. We've crafted this experience to be engaging, fun, and, above all, memorable. Yes, we'll cover the essentials like SELECT statements, JOIN operations, indexing, and more, but each lesson is presented as part of an epic quest, where every chapter is a new level. Every concept you learn and every challenge you overcome is framed within a series of interactive quests that mirror the excitement and depth of an adventurous role-playing game (RPG). By the time you reach the end of your journey, SQL will no longer feel like a series of commands—it will feel like second nature, a set of powerful tools you've mastered and can wield with confidence.

Your first quest may be something as simple as retrieving a list of legendary items from an ancient database hidden beneath layers of data forgotten by time. With each SELECT statement you craft, you'll peel back those layers, revealing artifacts long buried. As you grow bolder and more skilled, your adventures will take you deeper into the heart of SQLia, where you'll meet colorful characters—some friendly, some challenging—who will guide you, test you, and sometimes even compete with you, ensuring that your journey remains as dynamic as it is rewarding.

Let's break down what you can expect. In the beginning, you'll be introduced to the foundational concepts in a way that's easy to grasp, even if you've never written a line of code before. Think of it as learning how to wield a sword for the first time—awkward at first, but with practice, you'll soon become adept. From simple SELECT queries to more advanced JOINs and GROUP BY operations, every step builds on the last, creating a seamless learning curve that ensures you understand not just the "how" but also the "why" behind each command. By the time you're ready to face the final boss battle—a complex project that synthesizes everything you've learned—you'll have the confidence to not only solve problems but also adapt your solutions to fit real-world scenarios.

This book isn't just about memorizing commands or regurgitating syntax—it's about understanding. We've intentionally designed SQLia to teach you how to think critically and creatively about data. You'll learn not only the mechanics of writing queries but also the art of approaching data problems with a strategic mindset. Whether you're facing a dataset that seems insurmountable or a query that refuses to yield the right results, you'll develop the skills to approach the problem from different angles, testing hypotheses, refining queries, and ultimately arriving at a solution.

One of the hallmarks of this adventure is the balance between simplicity and depth. You won't need a background in computer science or programming to dive into SQLia. We start with the basics, making sure every step is clear and digestible, then gradually ramp up the complexity. By the time you reach the advanced sections, you'll find that you've built a strong foundation capable of supporting more complex ideas and techniques. It's like training for a marathon—at first, you take short, manageable runs, but soon, you're running miles without even realizing how far you've come. And when you reach the final stretch—the grand project that tests everything you've learned—you'll look back and see just how much ground you've covered.

Think of this book as your training ground, a place where you can hone your skills without the pressure of real-world consequences. Like any great adventure, the stakes in SQLia are high, but the environment is forgiving. You can experiment, make mistakes, and learn from them without fear. This is your chance to develop your SQL skills in a gamified, engaging setting where each challenge feels more like a puzzle to solve than an exercise to complete. By the end, you'll not only possess a robust set of SQL skills but also a deep sense of accomplishment, knowing that you've conquered the challenges and emerged victorious.

As you journey through SQLia, expect the unexpected. Some chapters may whisk you away to enchanted forests of nested queries, where each branch leads to deeper insights. Others may plunge you into the dark caves of data normalization, where strange beasts like anomalies and redundancies lurk, waiting to be tamed by your newfound understanding. You'll face bosses in the form of slow-running queries, complex datasets, and puzzling JOIN operations. And just when you think you've mastered one aspect of SQL, a new challenge will appear, pushing you to explore even deeper levels of understanding.

To keep your spirits high and motivation intact, we've infused the journey with plenty of humor and light-hearted moments. After all, learning something as powerful as SQL doesn't have to be a dry, monotonous slog through lines of code. Expect witty dialogue, quirky characters, and a few well-placed Easter eggs that will keep you entertained as you learn. These aren't just distractions—they're designed to make the lessons more memorable. Studies show that when you enjoy the learning process, you retain more information, and that's exactly what we're aiming for here.

Your journey through SQLia is more than just a technical exercise; it's a story you're a part of, and you're the hero. Every chapter is a step in your personal growth, and every challenge is a test of your newfound abilities. As you solve these puzzles, optimize your queries, and unlock the secrets hidden in the data, you'll gain not only knowledge but also the confidence to apply that knowledge in real-world scenarios.

The final boss of SQLia is waiting, but don't worry—you'll be more than ready by the time you reach that point. Whether it's writing a complex query that pulls together data from multiple tables, optimizing a sluggish report, or designing an entire database structure, you'll face the final challenge with the skills and confidence of a true data wizard. And as you cross the finish line, you'll not only understand SQL—you'll own it. You'll be ready to take on whatever challenges await you in the real world.

So, fellow adventurer, gather your wits and sharpen your mind. The road ahead is long, but it's paved with opportunities to discover, learn, and grow. Along the way, you'll face many tests, but each one will leave you stronger and more knowledgeable than before. And remember, every data wizard started where you are now—at the beginning of a grand quest. The heroes of tomorrow are born from the challenges of today.

It's time to step forward and carve your own path in the world of SQL. Adventure awaits, and with it, the keys to countless realms of data and discovery. Welcome to SQLia—let your journey begin!

CHAPTER 1

Introduction to SQLia

Your adventure begins in SQLia, a vast land where databases hold the key to knowledge, commerce, and even magic. To master SQLia, you must first understand its foundation—databases. These aren't just storage vaults; they're the lifeblood of kingdoms, guiding rulers, merchants, and wizards alike. Think of them as enchanted libraries, each filled with tomes that hold immense power. To tap into this power, you must know how to organize and retrieve information quickly and effectively.

What Are Databases?

In the world of SQLia, databases are as crucial as air and water. Without them, kingdoms would crumble under the weight of disorganization. To embark on your journey, you first need to understand what databases are and how they work.

Imagine a massive library—the Royal Archive of SQLia. Each row of shelves is organized with books (records), neatly categorized by subject and author (fields and columns). Now imagine that every time you needed a book, you had to manually search through thousands of volumes! Impossible, right? This is where the magic of SQL comes into play. With a simple spell (or SQL query), the librarian instantly retrieves the exact book you need.

But not all databases are alike. Some are highly structured, while others are more flexible and dynamic. Here's what you'll encounter on your journey:

Relational Databases (SQL)

The great libraries of SQLia, where every record is precisely cataloged. Relational databases use tables to store data in rows and columns, with clear relationships between different tables. Think of them as the royal archives, where the king's accounts and inventories are kept in perfect order. You'll use SQL, the language of the realm, to unlock these treasures.

Non-Relational Databases (NoSQL)

On the other side of SQLia lies the wild, bustling bazaars, where data is fluid and flexible. Here, records don't follow strict rules. Instead, NoSQL databases allow for a more chaotic but adaptable way of organizing information. They're perfect for handling vast amounts of unstructured data—like the merchants and traders of SQLia who rely on quick, ever-changing inventories. Imagine the stall owners at the Great Market, where the goods change every hour, and they need a flexible way to track their items.

Interactive Challenge – Choose Your Alignment: Will you be a loyal archivist of the Relational Kingdom, mastering the art of precise, organized data retrieval? Or do you prefer the chaotic energy of the Bazaars, where data flows freely, adapting to the needs of the moment? Write down your choice, brave adventurer, for it will guide your journey through SQLia.

Why Databases Matter

In SQLia, databases aren't just for keeping track of scrolls and books—they are the key to the prosperity of entire kingdoms. From commerce to diplomacy, everything depends on efficient data retrieval and organization. You, as the adventurer, will learn to wield this power to shape the future of SQLia.

Think of databases as the oracles of old, offering visions into the future. Businesses, governments, and guilds all rely on this data to make decisions. In the real world, databases are used to power social media platforms, e-commerce websites, and even healthcare systems.

For example, in the bustling city of Netflox, a mighty entertainment guild uses databases to recommend the perfect shows for its citizens. By analyzing viewing habits and preferences, they ensure that everyone has a magical viewing experience tailored to their tastes. Imagine being able to predict what someone will enjoy watching, all based on the data stored in a vast database!

Real-Life Analogy

When you shop online at an e-commerce site like Amazonia, every click you make is recorded in the site's database. This allows the merchants to suggest items you might want to buy, keep track of what's in stock, and even ensure fast deliveries—all thanks to the magic of SQL. And just like you'll learn to summon data in SQLia, merchants use queries to keep their kingdoms running smoothly.

Interactive Challenge: Spot the Database in Your Life: As you continue your journey, think about the databases you interact with every day. Is it when you log in to your favorite game or scroll through social media? How about when you check your bank account? Write down at least two examples of databases in your life and reflect on how they make your world more efficient.

Exploring SQLia's Kingdoms—Relational vs. Non-Relational Databases

Now that you understand what databases are, it's time to choose a path. SQLia has two great kingdoms—Relational and Non-Relational. Each kingdom offers different powers and strengths. Your mission is to explore both and decide where your loyalty lies.

The Relational Kingdom (SQL)

In the Relational Kingdom, everything is meticulously organized. Data is stored in rows and columns, and the relationships between these data points are crystal clear. It's like the grand archives of the SQLian castle, where every scroll (row) is carefully indexed and cross-referenced with other scrolls.

Here, you will use SQL—the language of the Relational Kingdom—to craft precise queries. If you need to find all the knights who have served for more than five years, you can summon that information with a single query:

```
SELECT * FROM Knights WHERE YearsOfService > 5;
```

In the Relational Kingdom, consistency and accuracy are prized above all else. Keys are used to link different tables, ensuring that data integrity is maintained. Imagine being able to link every knight to their noble house or every merchant to their guild, ensuring all information is accurate and interconnected.

The Non-Relational Realm (NoSQL)

But the Relational Kingdom isn't the only place to gain power. Beyond the walls lies the bustling Non-Relational Realm, where data is more fluid. Here, NoSQL databases rule. They are perfect for handling vast amounts of unstructured data, like the goods traded in the Great Market. You'll find merchants updating their inventories in real-time, with no need for rigid rules or structures.

Here, you won't need a strict schema. Document stores, key-value pairs, and graphs replace tables, making it easier to handle large amounts of unstructured data. For example, a merchant who needs to track sales might use a NoSQL database to record transactions, adapting quickly as the market fluctuates. In SQLia, the flexibility of the Non-Relational Realm offers an alternative way to manage data.

Your First Spell—Casting SELECT and FROM

Now that you've chosen your path, it's time to learn your first spell: SELECT. In SQLia, SELECT is the most fundamental spell, allowing you to retrieve data from any table in the kingdom.

Picture this: you've arrived at the Royal Library, tasked with retrieving a list of all the magical artifacts in the kingdom. You open your spellbook and cast:

```
SELECT * FROM Artifacts;
```

With a flash of light, all the artifacts stored in the database are presented before you! But there's more—SELECT can be as specific as you need it to be. Suppose you only want to know the names and powers of these artifacts. You'd modify your spell to:

```
SELECT Name, Power FROM Artifacts;
```

By casting this spell, only the information you truly need appears before you. SELECT is the backbone of data retrieval, and as you advance through SQLia, you'll use it in ever more powerful ways.

Navigating the Libraries—The Power of FROM

While the SELECT spell shows you what to retrieve, FROM tells you where to find it. The FROM clause is your map, leading you through the labyrinthine libraries of SQLia to the correct table.

If you want to retrieve data from the Royal Guard's Archives, for instance, you would cast:

```
SELECT * FROM RoyalGuards;
```

But if you wanted more specific data, like the names and ranks of the royal guards, you would cast:

```
SELECT Name, Rank FROM RoyalGuards;
```

By using the FROM clause, you ensure that your spell targets the correct table, pulling data from the right sources.

Interactive Challenge—Custom Spells: Now it's your turn, adventurer! Practice casting SELECT and FROM spells by creating your own queries. Try these:

1. Retrieve all the potions from the "Potions" table.

2. Pull the names and job titles from the "GuildMembers" table.

3. Extract the names and prices of all weapons from the "Armory" table.

Real-Life Scenarios—How Databases Shape SQLia and Beyond

SQL is more than just a magical language in SQLia—it powers the real world. In the Kingdom of Reality, databases are everywhere, from the websites you browse to the apps you use. Imagine a world where your favorite streaming service (Netflox) can recommend the perfect movie based on your previous choices. This is all powered by databases and SQL!

E-Commerce

When you shop online, every click and every item you browse or purchase is recorded in a database. This allows the site to recommend similar products and even remember what you left in your cart. It's just like the merchants of SQLia using data to improve their market strategy.

Social Media

Every time you post on FaceScroll or update your status, that information is stored in a massive database. SQL powers the algorithms that determine what posts show up on your feed, allowing for a highly personalized experience.

The Mystical Power of WHERE

As you journey through SQLia, you'll need to refine your spells to make them more powerful. Enter the WHERE clause. This spell allows you to filter your results, retrieving only the data that meets specific conditions.

For example, suppose you are tasked with finding all the knights in the Royal Guard who have served for more than five years. You would cast:

```
SELECT * FROM RoyalGuards WHERE YearsOfService > 5;
```

Now, you're only retrieving the data that matches your criteria! WHERE lets you filter out the noise, focusing your power on the data that matters most.

Sorting the Scrolls—ORDER BY

With your newfound skills, it's time to learn how to organize the data you retrieve. In SQLia, ORDER BY is the spell that allows you to sort your results in ascending or descending order.

Imagine you are in the Grand Library, sorting scrolls by the age of their authors. You would cast:

```
SELECT * FROM Scrolls ORDER BY AuthorAge DESC;
```

This would show the oldest authors first, descending to the youngest. Alternatively, to list the youngest first, you'd cast:

```
SELECT * FROM Scrolls ORDER BY AuthorAge ASC;
```

ORDER BY is essential when you need your results to be organized neatly—just like when arranging scrolls in a library.

Final Challenge—Can You Defeat the Data Dragon?

You've come far, adventurer, and now it's time for your greatest challenge yet: the Data Dragon. This fearsome creature guards the deepest, most valuable data in all of SQLia. To defeat it, you must retrieve information from multiple tables and use everything you've learned—SELECT, FROM, WHERE, and ORDER BY.

The Data Dragon demands you retrieve the names and ranks of all knights who have served for more than 10 years, sorted by rank. Can you craft the perfect spell?

```
SELECT Name, Rank
FROM RoyalGuards
WHERE YearsOfService > 10
ORDER BY Rank;
```

Congratulations, adventurer! You've defeated the Data Dragon and earned your place among the great heroes of SQLia.

Conclusion: The Journey Continues

You've learned the foundational spells of SQLia: SELECT, FROM, WHERE, and ORDER BY. These are your key tools for retrieving and organizing data. But this is only the beginning of your journey. In the next chapter, you'll delve deeper into the magical arts, learning to join multiple tables, aggregate data, and unlock even more powerful SQL queries.

Remember, adventurer, every query you write is a step toward mastering the magic of SQLia. As you continue your journey, keep practicing your spells and exploring the vast libraries and markets of SQLia. The more you learn, the more powerful you become.

Good luck, and may your data always be organized and your queries swift!

CHAPTER 2

Exploring the Fields of Data

As you go deeper into the world of SQLia, you find yourself in the heart of the Data Kingdom, surrounded by fields of information. Here, tables stand as mighty fortresses, housing the secrets of data within their walls. To unlock these treasures, you must learn how these structures work. But fear not, fellow adventurer—each table, column, and row is a coordinate on your treasure map, guiding you toward mastery over data.

In this chapter, you'll go into the foundations of databases, much like an explorer uncovering hidden cities. Each table you encounter is more than just a storage hub; it holds the keys to your SQL powers. Together, we'll reveal the mysteries of columns and rows, unlock the power of primary and foreign keys, and master the art of normalization. By the end of this journey, you'll be fully equipped to design databases like a true architect of the Data Kingdom.

Understanding Tables and Their Structures: Laying the Foundation

Tables are the lifeblood of databases—the enchanted vessels that hold and organize precious data, guiding your every query. Picture these tables as sprawling grids, much like the ancient maps pirates once used to find treasure. Each intersection of a row and column is an X, marking the spot where a unique piece of data lies waiting for discovery. But these aren't just static archives; they're active players in your quest, ensuring that data flows efficiently and remains easily accessible.

The Layout of the Treasure Map

Think of each table as a living, breathing structure made up of rows and columns. Columns (also called fields) are the treasure boxes that define what kind of riches they hold—whether names, dates, or golden coins (a.k.a. prices). Each row (also called a record) represents a single entry in your vast treasure trove, each one a unique collection of information waiting to be retrieved.

Imagine we are tasked with managing the data of our kingdom's citizens. You've built a table named "Citizen" with columns like CitizenID, Name, Email, and DateOfBirth. Each row represents one citizen—perhaps Sir Reginald, born on the fifth day of the Silvermoon Festival, with the email reginald@knightsmail.com.

But how do you distinguish one citizen from another in this growing kingdom? How do you make sure your treasure maps never mix up their markings?

Primary Keys: The Rulers of Uniqueness

Ah, Primary Keys—the royal decree ensuring no two rows are alike. Much like a royal crest, a primary key is a unique identifier that guarantees every record in the table has its own distinct identity. In our Citizen table, the CitizenID column would serve as the primary key, ensuring Sir Reginald and Sir Alistair never get mixed up.

Primary keys are your best friends when it comes to locating specific records in the blink of an eye. Like a magical tracker, they allow your database to find the exact row you're looking for without having to rummage through the entire table. Whether you're searching, updating, or deleting a record, the primary key ensures that your quest is swift and efficient.

Why Primary Keys Matter for Your Quest

Without a primary key, your data could fall into chaos, much like a kingdom without a ruler. Duplicate entries might sneak in, corrupting your records. For example, in an inventory system, you might end up with two identical items listed, making it impossible to distinguish between them. Worse still, trying to update or delete specific entries without a primary key could lead to errors, where incorrect rows are modified, resulting in data discrepancies.

Picture yourself as the captain of a ship, setting sail across the data seas. Without a clear heading—a primary key—you'd be adrift, lost in a sea of identical islands. But with a strong primary key, you can chart your course confidently, knowing you'll always find your way back to the exact location you seek.

Foreign Keys: Building Alliances Between Kingdoms

But what if you need to connect information from different realms? Enter the Foreign Key, a bridge that links one table to another, much like an alliance between kingdoms. A foreign key refers to the primary key in another table, forging relationships between tables and enabling you to connect data with ease.

For example, say you have an "Orders" table to track the purchase history of citizens. This table contains columns like OrderID, OrderDate, and CitizenID. The CitizenID here is a foreign key, linking back to the Citizen table, creating a relationship between orders and the people who made them. This ensures that every purchase is tied to a specific citizen, maintaining order and preventing chaos in the Data Kingdom.

The Role of Foreign Keys in Your Data Empire

Think of foreign keys as the royal messengers that travel between kingdoms, ensuring communication and unity. They create links between different realms of data, allowing you to explore complex relationships and build systems that span multiple tables.

Without foreign keys, your data could become disjointed and fractured, like scattered pieces of a broken mirror. Imagine trying to track customer orders without a clear link between the customer and their purchases. You might have an Orders table filled with data but no way to connect each order to the correct customer. By using foreign keys, you can weave these separate threads into a cohesive tapestry, ensuring that your data relationships are strong and reliable.

The Secret Art of Normalization: Keeping Your Data Pristine

In your journey through SQLia, you'll come across the ancient art of Normalization, a technique used to ensure your tables are pristine, efficient, and free of unnecessary clutter. Imagine a castle where every room is perfectly organized—each piece of furniture has a place, and nothing is out of order. Normalization does just that for your data, reducing redundancy and making your database perform at its best.

Let's take a look at some core principles of this magical practice:

- **First normal form (1NF)**: Every column must hold atomic (indivisible) values, and there should be no repeating groups. Imagine that your rows are knights—each knight should wield a single sword, not multiple weapons at once.

- **Second normal form (2NF)**: This ensures that all non-primary key columns depend on the **entire** primary key, not just part of it. Think of a royal court where everyone serves the king equally, rather than some subjects only obeying part of the throne's orders.

- **Third normal form (3NF)**: Here, every non-primary key must depend only on the primary key and not on other non-primary attributes. This is like ensuring every knight takes orders only from the king, not from the kitchen staff or court jesters.

By following these forms, you maintain clarity, improve performance, and ensure your tables aren't overrun with unnecessary information. Imagine a massive School database. Rather than cramming student details and their course enrollments into a single table, normalization splits these into two smaller, cleaner tables—one for Students and another for Enrollments. By connecting them with primary and foreign keys, you streamline your entire database, making it easier to manage and retrieve data.

Introduction to Columns and Data Types: The Tools of Your Trade

Now that you've mastered tables, it's time to equip yourself with another crucial skill: choosing the right data types for your columns. Think of this as choosing the proper tool for each task. You wouldn't use a quill to hammer in a nail, would you? The same principle applies to database columns—picking the wrong data type can lead to inefficiencies and errors down the road.

For example:

- **INT** (integer) is your go-to for numbers without decimals—ideal for counting citizens or tracking inventory.

- **VARCHAR** stores text-based data, like names or addresses—think of it as a scroll holding written records.

- **DATE** or **DATETIME** helps you track moments in time—perfect for logging when Sir Reginald joined the Knighthood.

By selecting the correct data types, you ensure that your columns behave predictably and efficiently, much like a well-oiled machine. But beware—choosing the wrong data type can lead to frustration. Imagine trying to perform calculations on a column that stores text instead of numbers—it would throw your queries into disarray!

Guarding Your Data with Constraints: The Royal Guard of Your Database

Just as a kingdom has laws to maintain order, your database has **constraints** that ensure everything remains in check. These constraints protect your data from chaos and corruption, much like the royal guard protects the castle.

The Most Trusted Guards

- **NOT NULL**: This constraint ensures that a column can never be empty—mandatory fields like primary keys or citizen emails must always have a value. It's like the royal guards making sure the gates to the castle are always manned.

- **UNIQUE**: As the name suggests, this ensures no two rows have the same value in a specific column, perfect for usernames or social security numbers. It's like ensuring no two knights in the kingdom wear the same suit of armor—everyone must be distinct!

- **CHECK**: This constraint allows you to enforce custom rules. For example, setting a CHECK constraint on an age column to make sure no one in your kingdom is recorded as younger than zero (no Benjamin Buttons here!). It's like ensuring every knight in your kingdom meets the age requirement for battle.

By using these constraints, you build a fortified database that protects your data from errors and inconsistencies, keeping everything orderly and reliable. With these guards in place, you can sleep soundly, knowing your data is safe.

Mastering the SELECT Spell: Querying Specific Columns

In the land of SQLia, the SELECT spell is one of the most powerful in your arsenal. It allows you to extract the exact information you need from your tables, much like consulting a magical tome for the answers to your quests. The syntax is simple yet elegant:

```
SELECT column1, column2, ...
FROM table_name;
```

If you want to know the first names and job titles of all your citizens, the query might look something like this:

```
SELECT FirstName, JobTitle
FROM Citizens;
```

You can retrieve specific columns or cast a wider net by selecting multiple columns. Imagine looking through a scroll filled with information about the entire kingdom—you can decide whether you want a detailed map (selecting specific columns) or a broad overview (retrieving all columns).

Using Aliases: Nicknames for Your Columns and Tables

Sometimes, it's helpful to give your columns and tables **aliases**—friendly nicknames that make your results easier to read. Much like a knight might be known by his title or deeds (e.g., "Sir Reginald the Bold"), aliases help you rename columns for clarity:

```
SELECT Revenue AS Total_Revenue, Cost AS Total_Cost
FROM Sales;
```

By renaming columns with aliases, you ensure that your results are easier to understand, especially when dealing with complex datasets. You're not just extracting data—you're crafting a narrative, guiding others through the story of your findings.

Designing Efficient Tables: Building the Kingdom's Infrastructure

Finally, no journey through SQLia is complete without learning how to design efficient tables. Crafting a well-structured table is akin to building a sturdy castle—it protects your data from invaders (redundancies, errors) and ensures the kingdom thrives.

Effective table design enhances data integrity, maintaining order in your kingdom's records. Redundant data can create confusion, leading to conflicts in your queries and reports. By enforcing unique constraints and ensuring each record has its place, you protect your data from chaos.

Understanding table relationships is also key to formulating queries that bring you the information you need quickly and accurately. Primary and foreign keys are like the roads connecting your kingdom's cities—without them, navigating from one table to another would be a nightmare.

Guidelines for a Robust SQL Castle

- **Plan ahead**: Think about the structure and relationships your data will need.

- **Normalize**: Reduce redundancy by organizing your tables into logical units.

- **Use constraints**: Protect your data by enforcing rules.

- **Test extensively**: Populate your tables and run queries to ensure they're working as intended.

Boss: The Guardian of Data Integrity

As you continue your journey through the Data Kingdom, you've conquered tables, mastered columns, and understood the secret arts of primary and foreign keys. You've even unlocked the ancient power of normalization, and now your path leads to the ultimate challenge—facing the *Guardian of Data Integrity*. This imposing entity stands between you and the ability to design efficient, scalable databases that ensure consistency, reliability, and flawless relationships between data sets. Only by defeating this final boss will you become a true architect of the Data Kingdom.

Boss Overview

The Guardian of Data Integrity isn't just any foe; it's a multidimensional adversary that tests your grasp of everything you've learned so far. Each of its attacks represents a different type of data integrity issue, from duplicate records to broken relationships between tables. The battle is not won through brute force but by demonstrating your mastery of database design principles.

The Guardian has four main forms, each representing a key aspect of database integrity: Unique Integrity, Relational Integrity, Domain Integrity, and Referential Integrity. You must defeat each form by solving challenges related to SQL principles. The boss will present you with real-world scenarios, and only the correct application of your skills will allow you to move forward.

Phase 1: Unique Integrity

The Guardian's first form represents Unique Integrity—the principle that ensures no two rows in a table are identical, particularly in fields where uniqueness is required. This form looms over a table filled with duplicate records and demands that you clean up the mess before moving on.

Challenge

"Adventurer, your task is to eliminate the threat of duplicate entries from this ancient table. I demand that no two records hold the same key! Prove your worth!"

- You are presented with a *Citizens* table containing duplicate entries in the *CitizenID* field, the primary key.

- The Guardian will attack your database with a chaotic blast of duplicate records, causing errors in querying.

Solution

You must summon the DELETE command to remove duplicates and protect the integrity of your database.

```sql
WITH DuplicateRows AS (
    SELECT CitizenID, COUNT(*)
    FROM Citizens
    GROUP BY CitizenID
    HAVING COUNT(*) > 1
)
DELETE FROM Citizens
WHERE CitizenID IN (SELECT CitizenID FROM DuplicateRows);
```

By purging the duplicate entries, you restore order to the table. The Guardian weakens, and the Unique Integrity form dissolves into mist.

Phase 2: Relational Integrity

Next, the Guardian shifts into its Relational Integrity form. This phase tests your ability to maintain meaningful connections between data stored in different tables. The Guardian severs these connections, leaving disjointed data scattered across your database.

Challenge

"Your connections between realms are weak! Repair the link between citizens and their orders, or lose the balance of your data kingdom."

- You must connect the *Citizens* table and the *Orders* table using the foreign key *CitizenID*.

- However, the Guardian has broken the foreign key relationships, causing inconsistencies between the tables.

Solution

Your task is to restore the link by setting a proper foreign key and ensuring that every order in the *Orders* table corresponds to a valid citizen in the *Citizens* table.

```
ALTER TABLE Orders
ADD CONSTRAINT FK_CitizenOrder
FOREIGN KEY (CitizenID) REFERENCES Citizens(CitizenID)
ON DELETE CASCADE;
```

With this action, any orphaned orders are removed, and the relational structure of the database is restored. The Guardian shrinks in size as the tables reconnect, but it isn't done yet.

Phase 3: Domain Integrity

Now, the Guardian assumes its Domain Integrity form, a glowing entity that guards the values within each table. This phase challenges your ability to maintain appropriate, valid data values in the database's columns.

Challenge

"Your values are in disarray, adventurer! A database without constraints is doomed to chaos. Show me that you can enforce the rules of your data fields!"

- The Guardian attacks by inserting incorrect data values into your *Citizens* table, such as negative ages and invalid email formats.

- You must protect your database by applying appropriate CHECK constraints and **NOT NULL** rules.

Solution

Deploy constraints to block the Guardian's corrupt data from entering your tables. Apply a CHECK constraint on the *Age* column and enforce NOT NULL on critical fields like *Email*.

```
ALTER TABLE Citizens
ADD CONSTRAINT chk_Age CHECK (Age >= 0),
ADD CONSTRAINT chk_Email CHECK (Email LIKE '%_@__%.__%'),
MODIFY Email VARCHAR(255) NOT NULL;
```

With these constraints in place, the Guardian's corrupted data bounces off the table's protective shield. The form of Domain Integrity flickers and fades, leaving you to face the final phase of the battle.

Phase 4: Referential Integrity

The final form of the Guardian is Referential Integrity, the most powerful and complex phase. This form ensures that relationships between tables remain unbroken, even when records are deleted or updated. The Guardian will attempt to break the connection between tables, leaving rows in one table referencing non-existent rows in another.

Challenge

"The ties between your tables are weak, and they will shatter under my power! Show me that you can maintain consistency across your database, or I will tear it apart!"

- The Guardian attempts to break the foreign key relationship by deleting records from the *Citizens* table that are still referenced by rows in the *Orders* table.

- Your task is to maintain referential integrity by ensuring that any deletion in the *Citizens* table cascades down to the *Orders* table, preventing orphaned records.

Solution

Implement cascading deletes to ensure that when a citizen is removed from the *Citizens* table, all corresponding orders are also deleted.

```
ALTER TABLE Orders
ADD CONSTRAINT FK_CitizenOrder
FOREIGN KEY (CitizenID) REFERENCES Citizens(CitizenID)
ON DELETE CASCADE;
```

By applying cascading delete rules, you ensure that the data in the *Orders* table remains consistent with the *Citizens* table. No orphaned records remain, and the Guardian's final form collapses under the weight of your carefully designed relationships.

Victory!

With the defeat of the Guardian of Data Integrity, you stand triumphant, having demonstrated your mastery over SQL's foundational principles. The tables in the Data Kingdom now function in perfect harmony, and your database designs are fortified against any threat of inconsistency or corruption.

As the Guardian dissolves into the ether, it leaves behind a glowing artifact—a *Key of Integrity*—symbolizing your newfound command over SQL. With this key in hand, you are now ready to build efficient, reliable databases that will stand the test of time. **Congratulations, adventurer!**

CHAPTER 3

The Quest for Precision—Filtering Data

In the enchanted world of SQL, filtering data is like wielding a magical lens that can sift through mountains of information, allowing you to find precisely what you're looking for. Imagine standing on a high peak, overlooking vast fields of data. With a swift command, your magic allows you to pinpoint the exact nugget of information you need hidden within the chaos below. In this chapter, we'll uncover the art and science of SQL filtering, learning to harness the power of the mighty WHERE clause—a skill that is pivotal for every adventurer in the realm of data analysis.

With your newly gained skills, you will soon be able to retrieve only the most relevant data, leaving behind all the noise and clutter. Imagine narrowing down customer orders to those placed in January or identifying employees who earn above a certain threshold. Your toolkit of SQL filtering techniques will soon become sharp and precise, ensuring your data queries are both efficient and accurate. Let's embark on this quest to master the tools of precision and strategy in the world of data!

The Sword of Precision: The WHERE Clause

As an adventurer seeking clarity in a world overwhelmed with data, you must learn to wield the WHERE clause—a blade that slices through the excess, revealing only the insights you seek. Filtering data effectively is the key to conquering the vast oceans of information that databases hold.

The Importance of the WHERE Clause

The WHERE clause is your sword, designed to narrow down query results with precision. Imagine you are a knight seeking the most valuable gems in a kingdom filled with stones. Without the WHERE clause, you'd be forced to sift through every stone one by one. With the WHERE clause, you can simply command the kingdom's guardians to show you only the gems that meet your criteria, saving time and energy.

Here's an example: Imagine you're managing a database filled with customer orders, and you need to find only the orders placed in January. Without the WHERE clause, you'd be forced to look through every single order—tedious and time-consuming. But with this magical tool, you can craft a query to summon only the January orders:

```
SELECT *
FROM orders
WHERE order_date BETWEEN '2023-01-01' AND '2023-01-31';
```

In this example, the WHERE clause filters out all irrelevant orders, leaving you only with the ones placed in January. It saves you from the cumbersome task of sorting through unnecessary data. In every database quest, mastering the WHERE clause is the first step to efficient data retrieval.

Understanding the Syntax Structure of WHERE Clauses

To use this sword effectively, you must understand its structure. The basic format of a WHERE clause is as follows:

```
SELECT column1, column2, ...
FROM table_name
WHERE condition;
```

The syntax begins with SELECT, followed by the names of the columns you wish to retrieve. The FROM clause specifies the table from which to pull the data, and finally, the WHERE clause defines the condition that each row must meet to be included in the result.

Let's say you want to retrieve data about employees who earn more than $3,000. The query would look like this:

```
SELECT employee_id, name, salary
FROM employee_data
WHERE salary > 3000;
```

This query ensures that only the rows where the employee's salary is greater than $3,000 are returned, effectively focusing the data retrieval process.

Practical Application Examples: Wielding the Sword

Let's move from theory to practice. Here are some real-world scenarios where the WHERE clause becomes your trusted companion in filtering data:

Finding transactions from a specific state: Suppose you have a dataset of sales transactions across various states. To filter only the transactions from California, you would use the WHERE clause like this:

```
SELECT transaction_id, amount
FROM sales
WHERE state = 'CA';
```

This command narrows down your data to only those transactions completed in California. It's simple, effective and targeted!

Retrieving customers based on age: If your dataset includes customer information and you need to find customers aged over 50, the WHERE clause helps again:

```
SELECT customer_id, name, age
FROM customers
WHERE age > 50;
```

Combining multiple conditions: In many quests, one condition isn't enough. You need to combine conditions using AND or OR to refine your search. For instance, to find male employees in California who earn more than $5,000 annually, your query might look like this:

```sql
SELECT employee_id, name, state, salary
FROM employee_data
WHERE state = 'CA' AND salary > 5000 AND gender = 'M';
```

With each condition linked by AND, only employees who meet all three criteria are returned.

Avoiding Pitfalls: The Dangers of Filtering

Even the most skilled adventurer must be wary of pitfalls. The WHERE clause, though powerful, can lead to errors if not handled carefully. Here are a few common mistakes:

Case Sensitivity

In many SQL implementations, string comparisons are case-sensitive. Searching for 'John' will not return rows with 'john'. To avoid this, use LOWER() or UPPER() to normalize text:

```sql
SELECT * FROM customers WHERE LOWER(name) = 'john';
```

Logical Operator Misuse

Be mindful of how AND and OR are used. A misplaced operator can lead to incorrect results. Use parentheses to ensure clarity in complex queries:

```sql
SELECT * FROM products WHERE (category = 'Electronics' AND price < 1000) OR (category = 'Books' AND price < 20);
```

Performance Issues

When filtering large datasets, performance can be a concern. Index the columns used in WHERE clauses to speed up queries. However, use indexing sparingly to avoid overhead.

The Arcane Power of Comparison Operators

To further enhance your precision, you'll need to master comparison operators such as =, <>, >, and <. These are the spells that allow you to filter data based on specific conditions.

Equals (=)

The = operator is straightforward: it checks if one value equals another. For example, to find customers named 'John':

```sql
SELECT * FROM Customers WHERE customer_name = 'John';
```

Not Equal (<>)

The <> operator works in reverse, finding rows where values don't match. To find all customers except those named 'John':

```sql
SELECT * FROM Customers WHERE customer_name <> 'John';
```

Greater Than (>) and Less Than (<)

To find sales greater than $100:

```sql
SELECT * FROM Sales WHERE sale_amount > 100;
```

Or to find sales less than $50:

```sql
SELECT * FROM Sales WHERE sale_amount < 50;
```

For more precision, you can combine these operators:

```sql
SELECT * FROM Sales WHERE sale_amount > 50 AND sale_amount < 150;
```

This returns sales amounts within a specific range, ideal for in-depth financial analysis.

Combining Conditions With AND and OR: A Balancing Act

AND and OR are your companions when filtering with multiple conditions. While AND tightens the grip, allowing only rows that meet all criteria, OR broadens the scope, including rows that meet any condition.

Let's break it down:

AND

Both conditions must be true. For example, finding employees aged 30 and working in California:

Sql

```sql
SELECT * FROM employees WHERE age = 30 AND state = 'CA';
```

OR: Either condition can be true. To find customers named John or living in California:

```sql
SELECT * FROM customers WHERE name = 'John' OR state = 'CA';
```

But real mastery comes when you combine **AND** and **OR**:

```sql
SELECT * FROM employees
WHERE department = 'D21'
AND (hire_date > '1987-12-31' OR salary > 50000);
```

The parentheses ensure SQL processes the conditions in the right order.

Common Pitfalls in Combining Conditions

As with any magic, there are dangers. Here are the most common mistakes when using AND and OR:

Missing parentheses: Without parentheses, SQL might interpret your query differently than you intended:

```sql
SELECT * FROM orders WHERE product = 'Laptop' OR product = 'Tablet'
AND quantity > 3;
```

This returns all laptops, plus only tablets where the quantity exceeds 3. Use parentheses for clarity:

```sql
SELECT * FROM orders WHERE (product = 'Laptop' OR product = 'Tablet')
AND quantity > 3;
```

Mismatched data types: Comparing incompatible data types (e.g., string to number) can cause errors. Always check that the data types match in your comparisons.

Incorrect operator usage: Double-check your logical operators to avoid mistakes. Misusing **AND** and **OR** can drastically alter your results.

Hands-On Practice: Sharpening Your Skills

To truly master the art of filtering data with SQL, practice is essential. Here are some interactive exercises for you:

Retrieve all sales above $500

```
SELECT * FROM orders WHERE amount > 500;
```

Find sales from January 2021

```
SELECT * FROM Sales WHERE DateOfSale BETWEEN '2021-01-01' AND '2021-01-31';
```

Find employees in department D21 with a salary greater than $50,000

```
SELECT * FROM employees WHERE department = 'D21' AND salary > 50000;
```

By practicing these, you'll enhance your querying skills, transforming complex datasets into valuable insights.

Final Thoughts: Becoming the Master of Data Filtering

In this chapter, we've unlocked the magic of filtering data using the WHERE clause. With this tool, you can slice through the overwhelming noise of large datasets and focus on exactly what matters. From mastering comparison operators to combining conditions with AND and OR, you now have the skills to navigate any data landscape with ease.

But remember, as with any magical tool, precision is key. Careful structuring of your queries, thoughtful use of parentheses, and diligent testing will ensure your success. Continue practicing and refining your techniques, and soon you'll be a master of data filtering, turning vast oceans of information into clear, actionable insights.

With this knowledge in hand, you're now prepared for the next challenge in your SQL adventure. The path ahead is filled with more advanced techniques, but with your trusty WHERE clause and newfound skills, you'll be ready to face whatever challenges arise!

But wait! While you're walking, a big shadow covers you. What's wrong?

Boss: Conquering Complex Filtering

Oh no! It's the boss of this chapter—a data puzzle so complex that only the most skilled SQL adventurer can solve it.

The Final Boss is not a villain in the traditional sense but a challenge of wit and logic. Your task is to conquer this boss by crafting a powerful SQL query that weaves together everything you've learned—WHERE clauses, AND/OR conditions, comparison operators, and aggregate functions. This test will push your abilities to the limit, but victory will bring you one step closer to SQL mastery.

The Boss's Challenge: The Kingdom of TradeMaster

The boss teleports you to the Kingdom of TradeMaster. Here you are the Royal Data Analyst, responsible for sifting through vast volumes of trade transactions, customer records, and product inventories. The King of TradeMaster is growing impatient. He demands a full report that summarizes the kingdom's trade activity, and only a perfectly crafted query will satisfy him.

Here are the requirements for your challenge:

1. **Find the most loyal customers**: You must retrieve a list of customers who have made more than five purchases AND have spent more than $1,000 in total across all their transactions.

2. **Highlight high-value transactions**: The King wants to know which products have generated the most sales. List all transactions for products that have generated over $5,000 in total sales.

3. **Special request for the king's birthday**: The King loves jewelry and electronics. He wants a list of all jewelry and electronics sold within the past six months, with transaction amounts above $500.

4. **Ultimate challenge—royal tax audit**: The royal tax auditors suspect there may be inconsistencies in recent transactions. You need to find all transactions where the amount exceeds $2,000, but only if the customer's total purchase history is less than

$10,000 (suspiciously high single transactions from otherwise low-spending customers).

This combination of queries is no ordinary task—it's a true test of your filtering skills, and the fate of the kingdom rests on your shoulders!

Conquering the Challenge: Crafting the Ultimate SQL Queries

Let's break down each of the boss's demands and build queries that will satisfy the challenge.

Part 1: The Most Loyal Customers

To find customers who have made more than five purchases and spent over $1,000 in total, you need to use both COUNT (to count their purchases) and SUM (to sum up the total amount spent). The query looks like this:

```sql
SELECT customer_id, COUNT(order_id) AS num_purchases, SUM(amount) AS total_spent
FROM orders
GROUP BY customer_id
HAVING COUNT(order_id) > 5 AND SUM(amount) > 1000;
```

In this query:

- **COUNT(order_id)** counts the number of purchases per customer.

- **SUM(amount)** calculates the total amount spent.

- **HAVING** is used to filter aggregated data, ensuring we only retrieve customers who meet both conditions.

Part 2: High-Value Products

To find the transactions for products that have generated more than $5,000 in total sales, you need to aggregate the sales amounts by product and then filter with HAVING:

```sql
SELECT product_id, SUM(amount) AS total_sales
FROM sales
GROUP BY product_id
HAVING SUM(amount) > 5000;
```

This query sums up the sales amounts for each product and then filters out any product that hasn't crossed the $5,000 threshold.

Part 3: Special Request—Jewelry and Electronics

For the King's birthday, you need to find all transactions involving jewelry and electronics that exceed $500 in value within the last six months. Use the OR operator to include both product categories and apply BETWEEN to capture the date range:

```sql
SELECT product_id, product_name, amount, sale_date
FROM sales
WHERE (category = 'Jewelry' OR category = 'Electronics')
  AND amount > 500
  AND sale_date BETWEEN CURDATE() - INTERVAL 6 MONTH AND CURDATE();
```

This query:

- Filters by the Jewelry and Electronics categories.

- Only includes sales where the amount is greater than $500.

- Uses the BETWEEN operator with CURDATE() to find sales in the last six months.

Part 4: The Ultimate Challenge—Suspicious Transactions

For the royal tax audit, you need to identify transactions where the amount exceeds $2,000, but the customer's total purchase history is less than $10,000. This requires a **JOIN** between the customer and order tables to calculate both the total spend and the individual transaction amount:

```sql
SELECT o.customer_id, o.order_id, o.amount, c.total_spent
FROM orders o
JOIN (
    SELECT customer_id, SUM(amount) AS total_spent
    FROM orders
    GROUP BY customer_id
) c ON o.customer_id = c.customer_id
WHERE o.amount > 2000 AND c.total_spent < 10000;
```

In this complex query:

- A subquery calculates each customer's total spend.

- The main query joins the order table with this subquery to find customers with total spending under $10,000.

- The WHERE clause filters for individual transactions above $2,000, satisfying the audit's requirements.

Victory: Defeating the Final Boss

Congratulations! You've conquered the Final Boss by completing all four parts of the King's request. You've shown your SQL prowess by using advanced filtering techniques, aggregate functions, and logical operators to retrieve precisely the data needed.

With your skills honed and your mind sharp, you're now ready to take on even greater challenges in the world of SQL. Remember, every query you write is a step further along the path to mastery. Keep practicing, keep refining, and soon you will be the true champion of the SQL kingdom.

As the King of TradeMaster rewards you with the highest honors, you are back in SQLia and leave the castle victorious, ready to tackle whatever data-driven challenges the future holds.

CHAPTER 4

Aggregating Adventures—Summarizing Data

Welcome back, brave adventurer! After conquering the realms of filtering data and grouping results, you're now ready to venture deeper into the mysterious caverns of SQLia, where hidden treasures await. This time, your quest is to harness the power of aggregate functions—COUNT, SUM, AVG, MIN, and MAX. These magical tools will transform the mountains of raw data before you into sparkling gems of insight. But beware, only those who truly master these abilities will unlock the deepest secrets of the data landscape.

In this chapter, you'll learn how to wield these aggregate functions with the precision of a seasoned adventurer. From counting your treasures to calculating averages and identifying the peaks and valleys of your data, these functions will help you discover hidden insights that were once buried in your datasets. But that's not all! You'll also encounter the mighty GROUP BY and HAVING clauses, which will allow you to organize and refine your newfound knowledge like a true data mage.

The Power of Aggregate Functions: Your Trusted Tools

As you embark on this journey, visualize each aggregate function as a magical artifact that will help you sift through the vast landscape of data to uncover invaluable treasures. Just as a skilled treasure hunter uses various tools to uncover hidden gems, these functions allow you to distill vast amounts of data into clear and actionable insights.

The COUNT Function: Your Treasure Map

The COUNT function is like a magical map that reveals the sheer scale of the treasure trove before you. It helps you see the vastness of the data by counting the number of rows that meet certain criteria. Imagine you've stumbled upon a vault filled with enchanted books—each representing a sale made by your company. You need to quickly count how many sales you made in a particular category, such as the legendary *Epic Fantasy* section.

Your Quest:

```
SELECT COUNT(*)
FROM books
WHERE genre = 'Epic Fantasy';
```

Suddenly, the treasure map reveals *100 books sold in the Epic Fantasy genre!* This insight allows you to understand the sheer volume of sales within that genre, helping you strategize your next move. Maybe you'll want to restock those popular fantasy titles or launch a special promotion.

Beyond the simplicity of counting rows, COUNT can be a powerful ally in identifying patterns and trends. Let's say you're running a large-scale survey for a kingdom-wide festival, and you need to count how many participants registered from each town. Using COUNT in combination with other clauses, you can uncover where the most eager festival-goers live, guiding you on where to allocate your resources for the festival.

Your Next Quest:

```
SELECT town, COUNT(*)
FROM festival_registrations
GROUP BY town;
```

The map now shows the bustling towns that can barely wait for the festivities to begin!

The SUM Function: Gathering Gold Coins

Next in your inventory is the SUM function, a powerful tool akin to a sack that gathers all the gold coins you've found along the way. SUM allows you to add up the numerical values in a specified column, giving you a total that can offer crucial insights.

Picture yourself as a merchant trying to calculate the total revenue from your coffee shop empire. You're staring at countless receipts from your sales across all branches. With SUM, you can gather them into one grand total!

Your Quest:

```
SELECT SUM(sales_amount)
FROM coffee_shop_sales;
```

With a flourish of your hand, the totals light up before you: *$120,000 in coffee sales!* Now you know just how much treasure your coffee empire has amassed this month. SUM is the perfect tool for revealing financial treasures hidden in your data.

SUM is especially powerful when you're dealing with large datasets. Imagine you're responsible for the finances of an entire kingdom, and you need to calculate the total taxes collected from different regions. The SUM function becomes your trusted ally as it tallies up the gold from each corner of the kingdom, giving you the full picture of your realm's financial health.

A Royal Quest:

```
SELECT region, SUM(tax_collected)
FROM kingdom_taxes
GROUP BY region;
```

With SUM at your side, the kingdom's treasury is revealed, and you can now decide which regions need more attention or where to invest for the future.

The AVG Function: Finding Balance

AVG is like the mystical balance scale of SQLia, giving you the ability to weigh out averages across your dataset. It's the tool that reveals the patterns hidden beneath individual numbers, offering wisdom to make informed decisions.

Imagine you're a time traveler tracking the average amount spent per transaction in your magic shop. You've been selling enchanted artifacts, but you're unsure whether the average customer is spending enough to keep your shop afloat.

Your Quest:

```
SELECT AVG(amount_spent)
FROM transactions
WHERE shop = 'Enchanted Artifacts';
```

With the flick of your wrist, the scales balance and reveal the answer: *The average customer spends $75 per visit.* This newfound knowledge helps you adjust your inventory or plan promotions to increase sales, bringing harmony to your business.

In a more complex scenario, imagine you're analyzing the performance of students at a wizarding academy. You want to know the average spell-casting score for each house to determine which house might win the coveted House Cup. AVG will help you find the trends and give you the insights to declare the winner.

The House Cup Quest:

```
SELECT house, AVG(spell_casting_score)
FROM student_scores
GROUP BY house;
```

Now, you have the insights to see which house is performing the best, allowing you to plan your next steps for training your young wizards!

MIN and MAX: The Scouts of Extremes

Your final tools are the agile scouts—MIN and MAX—who will help you identify the peaks and valleys in your dataset. Like a scout scouring the horizon for danger, MIN and MAX can show you the highest and lowest values at a glance, making it easier to navigate your journey.

Let's say you're in charge of managing a fleet of airships. You need to find out the fastest and slowest ships in your fleet to optimize your routes.

Your Quest:

```
SELECT MIN(speed), MAX(speed)
FROM airships;
```

The scouts return with valuable intel: *Your slowest ship flies at 200 knots, while your fastest soars at 500 knots!* Now, you can assign your fleet more efficiently, making sure your best ships are reserved for high-priority missions.

In another scenario, you're running an adventurer's guild and need to track the most dangerous quests based on the number of monsters defeated. You use MAX to find the quests with the highest monster count, allowing you to send your strongest adventurers to these treacherous lands.

The Adventurer's Quest:

```
SELECT quest_name, MAX(monster_count)
FROM quests;
```

Now you know which quests hold the greatest danger and which ones are safer for your less experienced adventurers.

Grouping Your Findings: The Art of ORDER and HAVING

With your new arsenal of aggregate functions, you can now group your findings into treasure troves of insight using the GROUP BY and HAVING clauses. Imagine you've uncovered piles of gold but need to organize them by region to understand where your riches are truly coming from. GROUP BY is your sorting spell while HAVING helps you set conditions to uncover only the most significant treasures.

GROUP BY: Organizing Your Loot

The GROUP BY clause is your magical organization tool. It allows you to group similar data into categories, making it easier to analyze the bigger picture. Imagine you're the treasurer of a kingdom, and you need to see how much revenue each town is bringing in. Without grouping, your data is scattered across numerous towns and difficult to interpret. But with GROUP BY, you can neatly organize the data and see the totals for each town.

Your Quest:

```
SELECT town, SUM(revenue)
FROM town_revenues
GROUP BY town;
```

With GROUP BY, the town revenues are now neatly organized, giving you a clear overview of the kingdom's financial landscape.

But what if you want to dive deeper? What if you need to know which towns have collected more than 10,000 gold coins in taxes? That's where the HAVING clause comes into play.

HAVING: Refining Your Search for Treasure

While the WHERE clause helps you filter individual rows, the HAVING clause is a tool you use after grouping data. It allows you to filter your grouped results, showing only the categories that meet certain criteria.

Let's say you've grouped the towns by their tax revenue, but you only want to focus on the towns that have collected more than 10,000 gold coins. HAVING will help you refine your search, showing you only the most profitable towns.

Your Advanced Quest:

```
SELECT town, SUM(revenue)
FROM town_revenues
GROUP BY town
HAVING SUM(revenue) > 10000;
```

With this powerful filtering spell, only the most prosperous towns appear on your map, allowing you to strategize for the future of your kingdom.

The Final Boss: The Maze of Complex Queries

Just as you think you've mastered the aggregate functions, a shadow falls across your path. The final boss appears—a monstrous maze of complex queries! To conquer this foe, you must combine everything you've learned so far.

Your task is to calculate the average sales of enchanted potions across all shops, group them by potion type, and only return the results for potions that have been sold in quantities greater than 100.

The Final Challenge:

```
SELECT potion_type, AVG(sales_amount)
FROM potion_sales
GROUP BY potion_type
HAVING COUNT(sales_amount) > 100;
```

You cast your query with precision, and the maze unravels before you, revealing the most popular potions in all of SQLia! Only those potions with significant sales volumes remain, allowing you to strategize for the upcoming potion fair.

But beware, the final boss has one last trick. He will throw massive datasets at you, hoping to slow you down. This is where optimization becomes key. You'll need to make sure you're indexing the right columns and using **WHERE** clauses to reduce the amount of data processed by **GROUP BY** and **HAVING**.

Handling NULL Values: The Phantom Data

As you prepare to exit the labyrinth, a mysterious figure appears—a phantom representing NULL values. NULLs are tricky, as they represent missing or unknown data, and they can wreak havoc on your queries if left unchecked. You'll need to handle these ghosts carefully, especially when using aggregate functions.

If you're working with a dataset that has NULL values, you may want to exclude them from your calculations or replace them with a default value. Let's say you're working with customer orders, but some of the customers didn't provide their location. You can use **COALESCE** to replace NULLs with 'Unknown' before grouping the data.

Your Quest:

```
SELECT COALESCE(customer_location, 'Unknown'), COUNT(*)
FROM orders
GROUP BY COALESCE(customer_location, 'Unknown');
```

With this spell, you've vanquished the phantom data, ensuring that your results are accurate and reflective of reality.

Conclusion: A Master of SQLia

With aggregate functions mastered, you stand tall as a true data sorcerer, able to see the patterns and trends hidden within the numbers. COUNT, SUM, AVG, MIN, and MAX have become your trusted allies, and you wield them with ease. As you continue your adventures, remember that these tools are not just about manipulating data—they are about uncovering the stories your data is telling.

By organizing your loot with GROUP BY and refining your search with HAVING, you've become a master of data analysis. You've faced the final boss and emerged victorious, using your skills to transform complex datasets into clear and actionable insights.

The treasure of knowledge you've gained through these functions is priceless. Now, armed with your new powers, you are ready to take on any data challenge that comes your way. The next time you face a labyrinth of data, remember that you have the tools to reveal the treasures within!

CHAPTER 5

Joining Forces—Combining Tables

Combining tables in SQL is like assembling a jigsaw puzzle—each table represents a piece of the picture, but when combined, they reveal a complete narrative. In this chapter, we'll journey through the various methods of joining data from multiple tables using different types of joins. These include INNER JOIN, LEFT JOIN, RIGHT JOIN, FULL OUTER JOIN, and even CROSS JOIN. Each join serves a unique purpose, offering different ways to uncover insights from your data.

Ready to unlock the mysteries hidden within your data? We'll start with INNER JOINs, revealing how they pull matching records from two related tables. You'll explore the syntax, practical examples, and common scenarios where INNER JOINs shine. Then, we'll move to LEFT JOINs, and RIGHT JOINs, demystifying their differences and showcasing when to use each. By the end of this chapter, you'll be equipped with the knowledge to choose the right join for any querying context, turning data into valuable insights. Buckle up for a fun, engaging adventure where SQL joins become your most powerful tools!

INNER JOIN: The Hero of Table Joins

Let's begin with the INNER JOIN, the hero of combining datasets. An INNER JOIN retrieves records with matching values in both tables. When you're working with normalized databases, where related data is spread across multiple tables, INNER JOIN helps connect the dots, allowing you to see the relationships between different datasets.

Basic Syntax of INNER JOIN

The basic syntax of an INNER JOIN is:

```
SELECT columns
FROM table1
INNER JOIN table2
ON table1.common_column = table2.common_column;
```

- **SELECT**: Specifies the columns you want to retrieve.

- **FROM**: Identifies the primary table.

- **INNER JOIN**: Specifies the second table to combine with the first table.

- **ON**: Sets the condition that defines how the tables are related.

For example, let's say you have two tables: Customers and Orders. The Customers table contains customer details, while the Orders table holds their purchase records. Both tables are linked by the CustomerID column. You can use an INNER JOIN to retrieve matching records:

```
SELECT Customers.CustomerName, Orders.OrderID
FROM Customers
INNER JOIN Orders ON Customers.CustomerID = Orders.CustomerID;
```

This query retrieves customer names along with their respective order IDs but only includes customers who have placed orders (i.e., records where there is a match between the CustomerID in both tables).

Real-World Examples of INNER JOIN

- **E-commerce**: You can use INNER JOIN to display customer orders by merging the Customers table with the Orders table. This allows you to show only customers who have made purchases.

- **Human Resources**: In an employee management system, INNER JOIN helps you generate detailed reports by linking the Employees table with the Performance_Reviews table.

- **Education**: In a school system, INNER JOIN connects student information from the Students table with their grades from the Grades table, ensuring that only students with recorded grades are included in the results.

Visualizing INNER JOIN

Imagine a Venn diagram with two overlapping circles—one for each table. The overlapping section represents the matching records that the INNER JOIN retrieves. Only rows that exist in both tables (where there is a match on the specified column) are returned.

INNER JOIN for Advanced Data Insights

Now that you understand the basics, let's explore more advanced uses of INNER JOIN. Suppose you want to pull data from three or more tables. For example, consider these tables: Customers, Orders, and Products. You can use multiple INNER JOINs to create a query that pulls data from all three:

```sql
SELECT Customers.CustomerName, Orders.OrderID, Products.ProductName
FROM Customers
INNER JOIN Orders ON Customers.CustomerID = Orders.CustomerID
INNER JOIN Products ON Orders.ProductID = Products.ProductID;
```

This query retrieves customer names, order IDs, and product names for every order placed. The ability to combine data from multiple tables allows you to see relationships across datasets, providing a comprehensive view of customer behavior and product performance.

LEFT JOIN and RIGHT JOIN: The Dynamic Duo

INNER JOIN is excellent when you need matching records from multiple tables, but what if you want to include data from one table, even if it doesn't match the other? That's where LEFT JOIN and RIGHT JOIN come into play.

LEFT JOIN

A LEFT JOIN retrieves all records from the left table (Table A) and any matching records from the right table (Table B). If there's no match, the result will still include the rows from Table A, with NULL values for columns from Table B. This is like saying, "Give me everything from Table A, and if there's a match in Table B, include that too."

Here's the basic syntax:

```
SELECT columns
FROM table1
LEFT JOIN table2
ON table1.common_column = table2.common_column;
```

RIGHT JOIN

A RIGHT JOIN is the opposite of LEFT JOIN. It retrieves all records from the right table (Table B) and matches them with records from the left table (Table A). If there's no match, you still get the records from Table B, with NULL values for columns from Table A.

```
SELECT columns
FROM table1
RIGHT JOIN table2
ON table1.common_column = table2.common_column;
```

Practical Use Cases of LEFT and RIGHT JOIN

LEFT JOIN in E-Commerce

Suppose you want to list all customers, even those who haven't placed any orders yet. You can use a LEFT JOIN to include customers without orders:

```
SELECT Customers.CustomerName, Orders.OrderID
FROM Customers
LEFT JOIN Orders
ON Customers.CustomerID = Orders.CustomerID;
```

In this query, every customer is listed, and customers without orders will have NULL in the OrderID column.

RIGHT JOIN in Project Management

Let's say you have a list of projects and a list of project managers, and you want to see all projects, even those without a manager. A RIGHT JOIN ensures all projects are included, with NULL for projects without a manager:

```
SELECT Projects.ProjectName, Managers.ManagerName
FROM Projects
RIGHT JOIN Managers
ON Projects.ManagerID = Managers.ManagerID;
```

This query lists all projects with NULL values for projects that don't have a manager.

When to Use LEFT JOIN or RIGHT JOIN

Deciding between LEFT JOIN and RIGHT JOIN comes down to which dataset is more important. Use LEFT JOIN when you want to prioritize the left table, keeping all its records. Use RIGHT JOIN when you want to prioritize the right table, keeping all records from it.

FULL OUTER JOIN: The Best of Both Worlds

Sometimes, you need the completeness of both LEFT and RIGHT JOINs. That's where FULL OUTER JOIN comes in—it returns all rows when there is a match in either the left or right table. If there's no match, NULL values are returned for non-matching columns from either table.

Basic Syntax of FULL OUTER JOIN

```
SELECT columns
FROM table1
FULL OUTER JOIN table2
ON table1.common_column = table2.common_column;
```

This type of join is especially useful when you need to combine datasets where records might be missing in either table, but you still want to see all possible data.

Practical Example of FULL OUTER JOIN

Let's say you manage a school, and you want to combine data from both the Teachers and Students tables. You want to see a list of all teachers and students, even if some students don't have a teacher assigned and some teachers don't have any students assigned. A FULL OUTER JOIN would return all records from both tables:

```
SELECT Teachers.TeacherName, Students.StudentName
FROM Teachers
FULL OUTER JOIN Students ON Teachers.TeacherID = Students.TeacherID;
```

This query lists all teachers and students, including those who don't have a match in the other table.

CROSS JOIN: Exploring Every Possibility

If you want to explore all possible combinations of two datasets, you can use a CROSS JOIN. A CROSS JOIN returns the Cartesian product of the two tables—essentially, it combines every row in Table A with every row in Table B.

Basic Syntax of CROSS JOIN

```
SELECT columns
FROM table1
CROSS JOIN table2;
```

Practical Example of CROSS JOIN

Imagine you're managing a restaurant and want to generate all possible combinations of menu items and drink pairings. You have two tables: MenuItems and Drinks. A CROSS JOIN will give you all possible menu and drink combinations:

```
SELECT MenuItems.ItemName, Drinks.DrinkName
FROM MenuItems
CROSS JOIN Drinks;
```

This query generates a comprehensive list of all menu items paired with every possible drink, giving you insights into potential combo deals.

Combining Joins: The Multi-Join Mastery

It's time to combine everything you've learned so far into a complex multi-join query. Let's say you're running an e-commerce business, and you want to create a report that combines data from customers, their orders, the products they purchased, and the departments those products belong to. Here's how you would write this multi-join query:

```
SELECT Customers.CustomerName, Orders.OrderID, Products.ProductName,
Departments.DepartmentName
FROM Customers
INNER JOIN Orders ON Customers.CustomerID = Orders.CustomerID
INNER JOIN Products ON Orders.ProductID = Products.ProductID
LEFT JOIN Departments ON Products.DepartmentID =
Departments.DepartmentID;
```

In this query:

- **INNER JOIN** is used to connect customers to their orders and products.

- **LEFT JOIN** is used to connect products to their departments, ensuring that even if a product doesn't have a department, it will still appear in the results.

This combination of joins lets you explore customer purchases, product details, and departmental information—all in one query!

Practical Applications of SQL Joins in Various Industries

SQL joins are powerful tools that can be applied across numerous industries. Let's explore how different sectors can benefit from joins:

Business Analytics

In business, you often need to combine sales data with customer information to gain insights. For example, an INNER JOIN helps identify relationships between customer profiles and their purchasing behaviors. A **LEFT JOIN** can help identify which customers haven't made purchases, enabling targeted marketing campaigns.

Healthcare

Healthcare providers can use joins to combine patient records with treatment histories. An INNER JOIN ensures that only patients who have received treatments are included, while a **LEFT JOIN** can identify patients who haven't received follow-up care.

Education

Educational institutions can use joins to link student data with academic records. INNER JOINs provide detailed reports that combine student profiles with their grades, helping administrators and teachers track academic performance.

Retail and E-Commerce

Retailers can use joins to analyze sales data and identify products that aren't selling well. A **LEFT JOIN** between products and sales data will reveal products with no sales, helping managers focus their efforts on underperforming items.

Boss: The Grandmaster of Joins Challenge

Welcome to the ultimate test of your SQL joining skills—the Final Boss of this chapter! You've battled through INNER JOINs, LEFT JOINs, RIGHT JOINs, FULL OUTER JOINs, and even ventured into CROSS JOINs. But now, it's time to put everything you've learned to the test in a multi-faceted challenge that will stretch your understanding and creativity.

The Grandmaster of Joins is here to challenge you with a real-world problem where you must combine multiple tables using different types of joins to extract meaningful insights. To defeat this final boss, you'll need to solve a complex data puzzle, showcasing your mastery of SQL joins in a comprehensive query.

The Scenario: The Ultimate E-Commerce Data Quest

You are the chief data analyst for a large e-commerce platform, and you've been tasked with creating a detailed report for the company's stakeholders. The report needs to combine data from several departments: customer information, orders, products, payments, and shipping. You'll need to use various joins to create a comprehensive overview of the business operations.

The stakeholders have three key questions:

1. **Customer orders**: They want to know which customers have placed orders, along with the product details and total amount they spent, including those who haven't made payments yet.

2. **Top products**: To prioritize shipping, they want a list of products that have been sold but haven't been shipped.

3. **Department analysis**: They need an analysis of the total sales per product category, regardless of whether or not products have been sold.

Let's break down the challenge and work through it step by step.

Step 1: The Customer Orders Report

For this step, you'll need to combine data from three tables: Customers, Orders, and Payments. You're tasked with retrieving a list of all customers, the products they've ordered, and their payment status. Even if a customer hasn't made a payment yet, they should still appear in the report.

Tables involved:

- Customers (CustomerID, CustomerName)

- Orders (OrderID, CustomerID, ProductID, TotalAmount)

- Payments (PaymentID, OrderID, PaymentStatus)

Here's your task:

- Use a **LEFT JOIN** to include customers who haven't made any payments.

- Use an **INNER JOIN** to link customers to their orders and product information.

```
SELECT Customers.CustomerName, Orders.OrderID, Orders.ProductID,
Orders.TotalAmount, Payments.PaymentStatus
FROM Customers
INNER JOIN Orders ON Customers.CustomerID = Orders.CustomerID
LEFT JOIN Payments ON Orders.OrderID = Payments.OrderID;
```

Step 2: Identifying Unshipped Top Products

Now, you need to help the operations team identify products that have been sold but haven't been shipped. This will allow them to prioritize shipping for those high-demand items. You'll need to join the Orders table with the Shipping table, but you also need to include products that don't have an associated shipping record yet.

Tables involved:

- Orders (OrderID, ProductID, Quantity)
- Shipping (ShippingID, OrderID, ShippingStatus)

To solve this:

- Use a **LEFT JOIN** to list all sold products, even those that haven't been shipped yet.
- Filter the results to include only products with a NULL **ShippingStatus**, indicating they haven't been shipped.

```
SELECT Orders.ProductID, Orders.Quantity, Shipping.ShippingStatus
FROM Orders
LEFT JOIN Shipping ON Orders.OrderID = Shipping.OrderID
WHERE Shipping.ShippingStatus IS NULL;
```

This query helps identify the unshipped products and ensures they are prioritized.

Step 3: Department Sales Analysis

For the final task, you need to analyze the total sales per product category, even for products that have yet to be sold. The stakeholders want to see every product category and the associated sales, even if some categories have zero sales.

Tables involved:

- Products (ProductID, ProductName, DepartmentID)
- Departments (DepartmentID, DepartmentName)
- Orders (ProductID, TotalAmount)

In this case:

- Use a **LEFT JOIN** to ensure all departments appear in the results, even if they don't have any associated sales.

- Use an **INNER JOIN** to link products with their orders, summing up total sales for each department.

```
SELECT Departments.DepartmentName, SUM(Orders.TotalAmount) AS TotalSales
FROM Departments
LEFT JOIN Products ON Departments.DepartmentID = Products.DepartmentID
LEFT JOIN Orders ON Products.ProductID = Orders.ProductID
GROUP BY Departments.DepartmentName;
```

This query provides a clear view of each department's sales performance, including departments without sales.

Bonus Round: Advanced Querying With Multiple Joins

The Grandmaster of Joins isn't satisfied just yet. Now, they challenge you to write a single query that combines all the above elements into one comprehensive report. Can you take on this final challenge and create the ultimate query that links customers, products, payments, and shipping details?

Here's what you need to do:

- Combine the **Customers, Orders, Payments, Products, Departments,** and **Shipping** tables into one comprehensive query.

- Include all customers, even those without orders.

- Include payment and shipping details where available.

- Summarize the total sales by department.

Here's how to build this query:

```
SELECT Customers.CustomerName, Orders.OrderID, Products.ProductName,
Payments.PaymentStatus, Shipping.ShippingStatus,
Departments.DepartmentName, SUM(Orders.TotalAmount) AS TotalSales
FROM Customers
```

```
LEFT JOIN Orders ON Customers.CustomerID = Orders.CustomerID
LEFT JOIN Payments ON Orders.OrderID = Payments.OrderID
LEFT JOIN Shipping ON Orders.OrderID = Shipping.OrderID
LEFT JOIN Products ON Orders.ProductID = Products.ProductID
LEFT JOIN Departments ON Products.DepartmentID =
Departments.DepartmentID
GROUP BY Customers.CustomerName, Orders.OrderID, Products.ProductName,
Payments.PaymentStatus, Shipping.ShippingStatus,
Departments.DepartmentName;
```

This query pulls together all the pieces of the puzzle: customers, their orders, products, payments, shipping details, and departmental sales. With this, you've successfully defeated the Grandmaster of Joins by mastering the art of combining multiple tables!

Victory!

Congratulations, you've defeated the Final Boss and completed the Grandmaster of Joins challenge! You've not only learned how to use INNER, LEFT, RIGHT, FULL OUTER, and CROSS JOINs but also mastered the art of combining data from multiple tables into cohesive, insightful reports. By completing these challenges, you've proven your ability to:

- Retrieve matching records with **INNER JOIN**.

- Include unmatched records with **LEFT JOIN** and **RIGHT JOIN**.

- Combine datasets comprehensively with **FULL OUTER JOIN**.

- Explore every possible combination with **CROSS JOIN**.

- Handle complex, multi-join queries that bring together data from across different departments.

You now have the power to tackle any data analysis task thrown your way. Whether you're working in e-commerce, healthcare, education, or any other industry, your mastery of SQL joins will allow you to unlock the hidden stories within your data.

Go forth, SQL Champion, and use your newfound skills to conquer new data challenges, uncover valuable insights, and become the go-to data hero in your organization!

CHAPTER 6

Unveiling the Hidden—Subqueries

Unveiling the hidden world of subqueries is like discovering a secret passage in the vast maze of SQL queries. These nested queries offer an elegant solution to simplify complex data retrieval tasks, turning what might seem like daunting challenges into manageable steps. By breaking down intricate logical sequences, subqueries make your SQL scripts cleaner and easier to understand, akin to finding a treasure map that leads you straight to the buried gold.

In this chapter, we'll explore how subqueries can transform your approach to writing SQL statements. You'll learn about defining and using subqueries, see practical examples of their application, and understand essential considerations for maintaining performance and readability. Whether you're calculating averages, filtering data, or constructing multi-step processes within a single query, this journey through subqueries will unveil techniques that enhance both the efficiency and clarity of your SQL coding adventures.

Defining Subqueries: A Key to Unlock Complex Solutions

Subqueries are like puzzle pieces that fit perfectly within your larger SQL query. They're queries nested within one another, helping to break down complex logic into smaller, more understandable parts. They're especially handy when you need to compute results temporarily without creating permanent tables.

Picture it like a nested treasure chest—each subquery sits inside the larger SQL query, adding a layer of precision to your results. Subqueries can live in clauses like **SELECT**, **FROM**, **WHERE**, or **HAVING**, making them versatile tools in your SQL kit.

Let's start with a simple example:

```sql
SELECT [Name]
FROM Production.Product
WHERE ListPrice = (
    SELECT ListPrice
    FROM Production.Product
    WHERE [Name] = 'Chainring Bolts'
);
```

Here, the inner subquery finds the price of 'Chainring Bolts.' The outer query then uses that result to retrieve all products matching the same price. It's like a magical spell that instantly fetches the exact information you're seeking without you having to sift through piles of data.

Pro Tip: Use subqueries to break down a long, convoluted query into simple, manageable steps, much like how you'd solve a maze by handling one section at a time.

Subqueries vs. Joins: Picking Your Weapon

Subqueries are powerful, but knowing when to use them and when to opt for joins is like deciding whether to wield a sword or a bow on your adventure. Both tools get the job done but in different ways. Let's compare:

Subquery Approach:

```sql
SELECT [Name]
FROM Production.Product
WHERE ListPrice = (
    SELECT ListPrice
    FROM Production.Product
    WHERE [Name] = 'Chainring Bolts' );
```

Join Approach:

```
SELECT Prd1.[Name]
FROM Production.Product AS Prd1
JOIN Production.Product AS Prd2
ON Prd1.ListPrice = Prd2.ListPrice
WHERE Prd2.[Name] = 'Chainring Bolts';
```

Both queries lead to the same treasure, but depending on your dataset's size, a join might be the faster route. As you continue your journey, you'll develop an instinct for which tool will serve you best—subquery or join.

Rule of Thumb: For scenarios where you need to eliminate duplicates or check for the existence of certain rows, consider if a join might yield better performance than a subquery.

How to Write Subqueries: Following the Map

Subqueries follow a basic syntax, always enclosed in parentheses to distinguish them from the outer query. You'll place them in **SELECT, INSERT, UPDATE, DELETE,** or other subqueries to make sure your SQL spells work flawlessly. Like any good map, it's important to follow the syntax rules to avoid getting lost.

For instance, subqueries can only contain an **ORDER BY** clause when a **TOP** clause is present. Keeping this in mind helps ensure your subqueries are properly formed.

The Secret Power of Subqueries

Using subqueries is like unlocking hidden doors in SQL that lead to clever shortcuts. They allow you to process multiple steps of data within a single SQL statement, reducing the need for temporary tables and minimizing complexity.

Imagine this: You run a bookstore and want to find which books are both bestsellers and highly rated. You could write two separate queries, but a subquery lets you bundle this logic into one sleek, powerful spell:

```
SELECT book_name
FROM books
WHERE book_id IN (
    SELECT book_id
    FROM bestsellers
```

```
)
AND rating > 4.5;
```

In one shot, you've simplified a multi-step task. Subqueries help you manage intricate logic, just as a compass helps you navigate a dense forest.

Correlated Subqueries: The Real-Time Oracle

Now, it's time to level up: welcome to correlated subqueries. These are like oracles that consult the outer query before making their predictions. Instead of running once, a correlated subquery re-evaluates with every row processed by the outer query, making it perfect for complex, context-sensitive tasks.

Here's an example of a correlated subquery:

```
SELECT employee_id, name
FROM Employees e
WHERE salary > (
    SELECT AVG(salary)
    FROM Employees
    WHERE e.department_id = department_id
);
```

The subquery recalculates the average salary for each department as the outer query evaluates each employee. Like a dynamic spell adjusting to new information, correlated subqueries allow you to handle complex conditions where relationships between data points matter.

Non-Correlated Subqueries: The Silent Companion

In contrast, non-correlated subqueries are silent companions—they complete their task independently of the outer query, execute once, and provide a fixed result.

Here's an example:

```
SELECT employee_id, name
FROM Employees
WHERE salary > (SELECT AVG(salary) FROM Employees);
```

The subquery computes the average salary once and then passes it to the outer query. It's like getting a static map of a city—you know exactly what to expect. Non-correlated subqueries are excellent for scenarios where the data doesn't change across each row.

Advanced Techniques: EXISTS, ANY, and ALL

Now that you've mastered the basics, it's time to delve into advanced techniques. These new tricks will make your SQL toolkit even more formidable.

EXISTS Subqueries

The EXISTS operator is like a scout in your SQL army—it checks whether a certain condition exists in the subquery, but it stops as soon as it finds a match. This can be much faster than counting all records or checking full results.

Example:

```
SELECT customer_name
FROM Customers c
WHERE EXISTS (
    SELECT 1
    FROM Orders o
    WHERE o.customer_id = c.customer_id
    AND o.order_date > '2023-01-01'
);
```

In this query, you're only interested in whether the customer has made an order this year. EXISTS ensures the subquery stops running as soon as it finds a match, keeping performance high.

ANY and ALL

These operators allow you to compare a value to any or all values in a subquery result. Think of them as magnifying glasses that help you zoom in or out depending on the number of matches you want.

ANY Example:

```
SELECT product_name
FROM Products
```

```
WHERE price > ANY (
    SELECT price
    FROM Sales
    WHERE sale_date > '2023-01-01'
);
```

In this example, you're checking if a product's price is greater than any of the sales prices in the current year. The query will return products where at least one match exists.

ALL Example:

```
SELECT employee_name
FROM Employees
WHERE salary > ALL (
    SELECT salary
    FROM Employees
    WHERE department_id = 2
);
```

In this query, you're checking if an employee's salary is greater than every employee in Department 2.

Practical Challenges: Gearing Up for Real-World Quests

Now, let's put these concepts to work with some challenges to test your SQL adventuring skills:

Challenge 1: Employee Performance

Create a query that lists employees who score below their department's average performance over the past six months.

```
SELECT emp_name
FROM employees e
WHERE performance_score < (SELECT AVG(performance_score)
                           FROM employees
                           WHERE department_id = e.department_id
                             AND review_date >= DATEADD(month, -6, GETDATE()));
```

In this challenge, you use a correlated subquery to adjust the average performance score for each department dynamically.

Challenge 2: Inventory and Restocks

You manage an inventory and need to find products with fewer than 10 items in stock, but only if they've been restocked in the last month.

```sql
SELECT product_name
FROM products
WHERE stock_quantity < 10
AND product_id IN (
    SELECT product_id
    FROM restocks
    WHERE restock_date >= DATEADD(month, -1, GETDATE())
);
```

This challenge uses a non-correlated subquery to filter for product IDs from recent restocks. Your reward? A clean, actionable inventory list!

Challenge 3: Customer Loyalty

You're tasked with rewarding customers who have made more than five purchases in the last year. Write a query that identifies these loyal customers.

```sql
SELECT customer_name
FROM Customers c
WHERE (SELECT COUNT(*)
       FROM Orders o
       WHERE o.customer_id = c.customer_id
       AND o.order_date >= DATEADD(year, -1, GETDATE())) > 5;
```

Here, you use a correlated subquery to dynamically count purchases per customer and check against the loyalty threshold.

Advanced Performance Optimization for Subqueries

As you climb the SQL mountain, you'll encounter larger datasets and more complex queries. Subqueries are powerful, but they can slow down if not used wisely. Let's explore some techniques to keep your queries lightning-fast.

Indexing for Faster Subqueries

Indexing is like turbocharging your SQL engine. By creating indexes on columns used in subqueries, you help SQL find data faster. Without an index, SQL has to scan through every row to find the right match—a tedious process.

For example, if you frequently filter based on customer_id in subqueries, indexing this column ensures faster lookups:

```sql
CREATE INDEX idx_customer_id ON Orders (customer_id);
```

This small step drastically reduces query execution time, especially for large datasets.

Converting Correlated Subqueries to Joins

Correlated subqueries re-run for every row, which can slow down performance, especially with big tables. In many cases, converting them into joins speeds things up. Here's an example:

Correlated Subquery:

```sql
SELECT emp_name
FROM Employees e
WHERE salary > (
    SELECT AVG(salary)
    FROM Employees
    WHERE e.department_id = department_id
);
```

Equivalent Join:

```sql
SELECT e.emp_name
FROM Employees e
JOIN (
    SELECT department_id, AVG(salary) AS avg_salary
    FROM Employees
    GROUP BY department_id
) AS avg_salaries
ON e.department_id = avg_salaries.department_id
WHERE e.salary > avg_salaries.avg_salary;
```

The join reduces redundant operations, making the query faster.

Temporary Tables and Common Table Expressions (CTEs)

Another method for optimizing subqueries is by using temporary tables or CTEs. By storing intermediate results, you eliminate the need to recompute subqueries.

Example using a CTE:

```sql
WITH AvgSalaries AS (
    SELECT department_id, AVG(salary) AS avg_salary
    FROM Employees
    GROUP BY department_id
)
SELECT e.emp_name
FROM Employees e
JOIN AvgSalaries a
ON e.department_id = a.department_id
WHERE e.salary > a.avg_salary;
```

By using a CTE, SQL computes the average salary once and then joins it with the main query, speeding up execution.

Boss Battle: Complex Subqueries

Your final challenge as an SQL adventurer is to conquer a complex, multi-step query that requires subqueries, joins, and optimization. Are you ready?

Final Challenge: Department Performance Review

Your company wants a detailed report of all departments, listing each department's name, its manager, the total number of employees, and the department's average salary. However, you only want departments where the average salary exceeds the company-wide average.

Here's your solution:

```sql
WITH CompanyAvg AS (
    SELECT AVG(salary) AS company_avg_salary
    FROM Employees
),
DeptDetails AS (
```

```
    SELECT d.department_name, m.manager_name, COUNT(e.employee_id) AS
total_employees, AVG(e.salary) AS dept_avg_salary
    FROM Departments d
    JOIN Employees e ON d.department_id = e.department_id
    JOIN Managers m ON d.manager_id = m.manager_id
    GROUP BY d.department_name, m.manager_name
)
SELECT department_name, manager_name, total_employees, dept_avg_salary
FROM DeptDetails
WHERE dept_avg_salary > (SELECT company_avg_salary FROM CompanyAvg);
```

This complex query combines a CTE, joins, and a subquery to filter departments based on salary. Your final reward? Mastery of SQL subqueries!

Final Thoughts: Becoming a Subquery Master

As you venture deeper into the SQL world, subqueries will become one of your most reliable tools, helping you simplify complex logic and navigate even the trickiest data landscapes. They're elegant, powerful, and flexible—just what every data adventurer needs.

But remember, with great power comes great responsibility. Be mindful of performance impacts, especially when using correlated subqueries on large datasets. With practice, you'll learn when to wield them for maximum impact, turning every query into a smooth and efficient SQL operation.

So continue exploring, experiment with different subqueries, and let your newfound skills guide you through the wild terrains of SQL. Who knows? You might even uncover the next hidden treasure.

CHAPTER 7

Data Wizards—Functions and Expressions

Harnessing the power of SQL functions can transform your data manipulation skills into a form of wizardry, making complex queries more efficient and effective. Imagine having a toolkit filled with magical spells that can simplify tasks, improve performance, and present data in ways you never thought possible. These built-in SQL functions are like those very spells, turning even the most convoluted tasks into straightforward commands that yield precise results.

In this chapter, you'll dive deep into the world of SQL functions, exploring how they can significantly enhance your query performance and streamline your workflow. You'll learn about various string functions, such as **CONCAT** for combining text fields, LENGTH for validating data lengths, and **SUBSTR** for extracting specific segments of text. As you journey further, you'll unlock the secrets of date functions that handle temporal data with ease, and mathematical functions that simplify complex calculations. By the end of this chapter, you'll be well-equipped to wield these powerful tools, transforming raw data into meaningful insights with the finesse of a true data wizard.

String Functions: CONCAT, LENGHT, SUBSTR

When diving into the realm of SQL, one can't overlook the importance of string functions. These powerful tools allow for effective manipulation and retrieval of text data, enabling us to craft precise queries that can simplify data management and analysis. Let's explore some vital string functions: **CONCAT**, **LENGTH**, and **SUBSTR**, each serving unique purposes in handling text data efficiently.

CONCAT: Combining Strings for Enhanced Data Output

First up is the **CONCAT** function. The primary role of **CONCAT** is to combine multiple strings into a single cohesive string. This capability is particularly handy when dealing with separate fields that need to be presented as a unified entity. For instance, consider a database containing customer information split into separate fields for first and last names. If you want to display the full names of customers in your reports or user interface, the **CONCAT** function becomes indispensable.

Imagine you have a table named **customers** with columns **first_name** and **last_name**. By using the **CONCAT** function, you can create a new column, **full_name**, that combines these two fields. The query would look something like this:

```
SELECT customer_id, CONCAT(first_name, ' ', last_name) AS full_name
FROM customers;
```

Here, the **CONCAT** function takes the **first_name** and **last_name** values, adds a space between them, and forms a new string stored in the **full_name** column. This makes the data more readable and easier to work with, especially when generating reports or performing further data analysis. The utility of **CONCAT** doesn't stop there; it encourages creativity in reporting and data presentation by allowing users to format text in engaging ways. For instance, you could format addresses for mailing labels or concatenate multiple fields for form submissions.

A more advanced use case of **CONCAT** can be seen when generating personalized emails for a marketing campaign. Suppose you want to send out custom greetings by combining a person's title (e.g., "Mr." or "Ms.") with their full name:

```
SELECT CONCAT(title, ' ', first_name, ' ', last_name, ', welcome to
our service!') AS greeting
FROM customers;
```

In this query, we dynamically generate personalized greetings, ensuring that each customer receives a uniquely crafted message. The power of **CONCAT** lies not only in its ability to join fields but also in the flexibility to include static text or symbols to create customized outputs that meet your business needs.

LENGTH: Ensuring Data Integrity through String Length Validation

Next, we turn our attention to the **LENGTH** function. This function returns the length of a given string, which can be incredibly useful for data validation and compliance checking. For instance, if a business rule specifies that certain data fields must not exceed a specific length, the **LENGTH** function helps ensure that these rules are adhered to.

Let's say you need to validate the length of customer names to ensure they do not surpass a set limit. You could use a query like this:

```
SELECT customer_id, full_name, LENGTH(full_name) AS name_length FROM customers;
```

In this example, the **LENGTH** function calculates the number of characters in the **full_name** field and stores this value in the **name_length** column. This is essential for maintaining data consistency and integrity, particularly when dealing with systems that impose strict formatting rules, such as credit card numbers or international phone numbers.

Imagine you're working on a shipping application that requires ZIP codes to be exactly five digits. By using the **LENGTH** function, you can filter out invalid entries and notify users to correct their input:

```
SELECT address_id, zip_code
FROM addresses
WHERE LENGTH(zip_code) != 5;
```

This query highlights all addresses with incorrectly formatted ZIP codes, making it easier for users or administrators to identify and correct mistakes. The LENGTH function, therefore, plays a crucial role in maintaining the accuracy of your dataset.

Moreover, the **LENGTH** function is highly valuable for analyzing unstructured data. For example, in a social media context, it could be used to ensure that posts or comments adhere to character limits, which might be imposed to improve readability or user experience.

SUBSTR: Extracting the Most Relevant Data

Finally, let's dive into the **SUBSTR** function, a versatile tool that extracts a substring from a given string based on a specified starting position and length. This function proves valuable in scenarios where only a portion of a string is needed for analysis or reporting. For instance, suppose you need to extract area codes from phone numbers stored in a database.

Consider a table **contacts** with a column **phone_number** containing phone numbers in the format **123-456-7890**. To extract the first three digits representing the area code, you could use the following query:

```
SELECT contact_id, phone_number, SUBSTR(phone_number, 1, 3) AS
area_code FROM contacts;
```

Here, the **SUBSTR** function takes the **phone_number** string and starts extraction at position 1, continuing for 3 characters, thereby isolating the area code. This ability to focus on key portions of strings is invaluable for various analytical tasks, such as categorizing data based on geographical regions or filtering records according to specific criteria.

In more advanced use cases, **SUBSTR** can be combined with other functions to manipulate and reformat strings for specialized outputs. For instance, you might use **SUBSTR** in combination with the **CONCAT** function to extract and reformat dates stored as strings:

```
SELECT CONCAT(SUBSTR(date_field, 6, 2), '/', SUBSTR(date_field, 9, 2),
'/', SUBSTR(date_field, 1, 4)) AS formatted_date
FROM events;
```

This query extracts different parts of a date in **YYYY-MM-DD** format and reformats it to the more familiar **MM/DD/YYYY** format. Such manipulation can be crucial when generating reports or converting data for use in other systems that require specific formats.

To summarize, string functions like **CONCAT**, **LENGTH**, and **SUBSTR** offer robust mechanisms for manipulating and retrieving text data in SQL. They enable the creation of cohesive data outputs, ensure compliance with business rules through validation, and focus on critical portions of strings for detailed analysis. Mastering these functions enhances your ability to craft precise and efficient SQL queries, ultimately leading to better data management and insightful analysis.

Date Functions: NOW, DATE_ADD, DATEDIFF

Mastering date functions is like wielding a magical spell to manage and analyze temporal data efficiently. These functions are indispensable for anyone who wishes to elevate their SQL prowess and make data-driven decisions with precision.

Let's dive into three fundamental date functions: **NOW**, **DATE_ADD**, and **DATEDIFF**. Each of these plays a pivotal role in handling temporal data, from timestamping records to calculating future dates and analyzing durations.

NOW: Capturing the Present Moment

First up, the **NOW** function. This powerful tool retrieves the current date and time, making it an essential component for real-time data analysis. Imagine you're working on a sales dashboard that needs to reflect the most current data. By using the **NOW** function, you can ensure that your timestamps are precise, facilitating accurate decision-making.

For example, when inserting a new record into a table, you might use:

```sql
INSERT INTO sales (product_id, quantity, sale_date)
VALUES (101, 5, NOW());
```

This simple yet effective function stamps each sale record with the exact moment it was created, which is crucial for auditing, logging events, or any scenario where timing is everything. The **NOW** function can also be used in broader reporting contexts where real-time analysis is critical, such as generating end-of-day reports:

```sql
SELECT SUM(total_sales) AS daily_sales
FROM sales
WHERE sale_date = DATE(NOW());
```

In this query, **NOW()** ensures that only today's sales are included, making it easier to monitor performance or identify trends as they happen.

DATE_ADD: Projecting into the Future

Next, we have the **DATE_ADD** function, which adds a specified interval to a date. This is particularly useful in project management and deadline tracking, as it enables users to calculate future dates without manual adjustments. Say you're managing a software development project with multiple sprints. To find out when the next sprint starts, you could use:

```
SELECT DATE_ADD(CURDATE(), INTERVAL 14 DAY) AS next_sprint_start;
```

Here, **CURDATE()** returns today's date, and **DATE_ADD** adds 14 days to it, giving you the start date of the next sprint. This eliminates the tedious task of manually counting days on a calendar, ensuring consistent and error-free scheduling.

But **DATE_ADD** isn't just limited to days. You can use it to add any unit of time, from seconds to years. For instance, suppose you're working on an annual subscription service and need to calculate when a customer's subscription will expire. Using **DATE_ADD**, you can easily calculate expiration dates based on the subscription start date:

```
SELECT customer_id, DATE_ADD(start_date, INTERVAL 1 YEAR) AS
expiration_date
FROM subscriptions;
```

In this scenario, **DATE_ADD** ensures that each customer's subscription is extended by exactly one year, with no need for manual tracking or adjustments.

DATEDIFF: Measuring Durations and Time Gaps

Finally, there's the **DATEDIFF** function, which calculates the difference between two dates. This function is invaluable for gaining insights into durations or time intervals, whether for sales, projects, or personal metrics analysis. For instance, if you want to determine how long a particular promotional campaign ran, you could leverage this function as follows:

```
SELECT DATEDIFF(end_date, start_date) AS campaign_duration
FROM promotions
WHERE promo_id = 202;
```

By subtracting the **start_date** from the **end_date**, **DATEDIFF** yields the campaign duration in days, enabling you to assess performance over time. Whether comparing sales periods or tracking project milestones, understanding durations is critical for strategic planning and optimization.

DATEDIFF is also helpful in analyzing customer behavior. Suppose you want to measure the average time between customer purchases to identify loyal customers or those who might be at risk of churn. You could use **DATEDIFF** to calculate the number of days between successive purchases:

```
SELECT customer_id, DATEDIFF(MAX(purchase_date), MIN(purchase_date))
AS days_between_purchases
FROM purchases
GROUP BY customer_id;
```

This query calculates the time gap between the earliest and most recent purchases for each customer, offering insights into purchase patterns and helping businesses design targeted marketing strategies.

Combining Date Functions: A Holistic Example

To further illustrate the utility of date functions, let's consider a comprehensive example combining all three. Suppose you're overseeing a subscription service and need to generate a report showcasing user engagement over the past month. You might write:

```
SELECT user_id, signup_date,
DATE_ADD(signup_date, INTERVAL 30 DAY) AS one_month_anniversary,
DATEDIFF(NOW(), signup_date) AS days_since_signup
FROM users
WHERE signup_date BETWEEN DATE_SUB(NOW(), INTERVAL 1 MONTH) AND NOW();
```

In this query, signup_date marks when each user joined. Using DATE_ADD, you calculate their one-month anniversary and DATEDIFF determines how many days have elapsed since they signed up. Combining these functions provides a holistic view of user activity within the desired timeframe, enabling you to identify trends or opportunities for re-engagement campaigns.

Real-World Use Cases of Date Functions

Imagine another scenario where these functions shine: e-commerce analytics. For instance, an online store wants to offer personalized discounts based on customers' anniversaries of their first purchase. Implementing this involves several steps facilitated by our beloved date functions. First, extract the customers who have their purchase anniversary in the upcoming week:

```
SELECT customer_id, first_purchase_date,
DATE_ADD(first_purchase_date, INTERVAL YEAR(NOW()) -
YEAR(first_purchase_date) YEAR) AS this_year_anniversary
FROM orders
WHERE DATE_ADD(first_purchase_date, INTERVAL YEAR(NOW()) -
YEAR(first_purchase_date) YEAR)
BETWEEN NOW() AND DATE_ADD(NOW(), INTERVAL 7 DAY);
```

Here, first_purchase_date gives the initial purchase date. The DATE_ADD function aligns the anniversary to the current year, and the WHERE clause filters for those whose anniversaries fall within the next seven days. This allows the marketing team to prepare personalized messages or discounts, increasing the likelihood of customer retention and engagement.

In a corporate setting, project management teams might use the NOW and DATE_ADD functions to track deadlines or set future milestones. For example, to track when a team's next review is due, they could use:

```
SELECT project_id, project_name,
DATE_ADD(review_date, INTERVAL 90 DAY) AS next_review_date
FROM projects;
```

This query adds 90 days to each project's last review date to determine when the next review should occur. Automating these kinds of calculations ensures no important milestones are missed, allowing for smoother project execution.

Finally, consider corporate event management. Tracking the duration of employee training sessions across different departments can be streamlined using these date functions. Suppose HR wants to measure the effectiveness of recent training by comparing completion times across various teams:

```
SELECT employee_id, department, DATEDIFF(training_end_date,
training_start_date) AS training_duration
FROM employee_training
ORDER BY department;
```

In this query, DATEDIFF calculates the number of days each training session lasted. Sorting by department allows HR to analyze durations and identify potential bottlenecks or areas needing improvement.

To summarize, SQL's NOW, DATE_ADD, and DATEDIFF functions serve as your toolkit for adeptly managing temporal data. Whether you're timestamping records for real-time analysis, calculating future dates for project timelines, or determining the length of promotional campaigns, these functions provide robust solutions to everyday challenges.

Mathematical Functions: ABS, ROUND, POWER

Mathematical functions are essential tools in SQL for performing various calculations and transformations on numerical data. These functions not only simplify complex tasks but also enhance the efficiency and accuracy of data analysis. Let's explore three key mathematical functions—**ABS**, **ROUND**, and **POWER**—and understand how they can be utilized effectively within SQL queries.

ABS: Handling Negative Numbers and Variances

The **ABS** function is indispensable when dealing with negative numbers in data analysis. It returns the absolute value of a number, effectively transforming any negative value into its positive counterpart. This function is particularly useful in scenarios where the magnitude of a number is more important than its sign.

Consider a scenario where we need to calculate the difference between predicted and actual sales performance. Negative differences might indicate underperformance, but for some analyses, we're only interested in the size of the difference. By applying the ABS function, we ensure that all differences are treated as positive values, simplifying further calculations.

For example:

```
SELECT ABS(predicted_sales - actual_sales) AS sales_diff
FROM sales_data;
```

In this query, the **ABS** function calculates the absolute difference between the predicted and actual sales figures, ensuring accurate and meaningful analysis regardless of whether the performance was above or below expectations.

Another practical use of the **ABS** function is in financial data analysis. For instance, imagine preparing a dashboard showcasing the historical performance of a stock. The finance team might request the absolute difference between the opening and closing prices for each trading day. This is achieved by using:

```
SELECT ABS(closing_price - opening_price) AS price_diff
FROM stock_prices;
```

By leveraging the **ABS** function here, analysts obtain clear insights into the daily price movements without worrying about the direction of change.

ROUND: Ensuring Precision in Financial and Statistical Reporting

Precision in numerical data is paramount, especially in financial reporting and analytics. The **ROUND** function comes to the rescue by allowing us to round a number to a specified number of decimal places, making data more interpretable and presentable.

Imagine you are compiling a report displaying the average closing prices of stocks over a year. Raw data might have closing prices with numerous decimal places, which can be unwieldy and hard to read. Using the **ROUND** function, you can control the level of precision, ensuring the numbers are easy to interpret.

Here's an example:

```
SELECT ROUND(AVG(closing_price), 2) AS avg_price
FROM stock_data;
```

In this query, the **ROUND** function rounds the average closing price to two decimal places, making the resulting figure more readable and suitable for reports.

Financial statements often require precise figures rounded to a specific number of decimal places to maintain consistency and clarity. For example, while calculating quarterly revenue growth percentages, rounding the results ensures that stakeholders quickly grasp the trends without getting bogged down by excessive digits.

Consider another example:

```
SELECT ROUND(quarterly_revenue * 0.05, 2) AS growth_projection
FROM financial_reports;
```

Here, we project future growth based on current quarterly revenues and round the result to two decimal places, which is crucial for clear communication in financial summaries.

POWER: Empowering Advanced Calculations and Forecasts

The **POWER** function elevates SQL's capability by allowing exponential calculations directly within your queries. This function raises a number to the power of a specified exponent, facilitating advanced mathematical modeling without the need for external tools like spreadsheets or programming languages.

One of the most common applications of the **POWER** function is in financial forecasting. Suppose you want to calculate compound interest, which involves raising a base amount to the power representing the number of compounding periods. The **POWER** function streamlines this calculation.

For example:

```
SELECT initial_amount * POWER(1 + interest_rate, periods) AS
compound_interest
FROM investments;
```

In this query, **POWER** efficiently calculates the compound interest, demonstrating its utility in financial mathematics.

The **POWER** function also finds relevance in scientific and engineering applications. Consider a scenario where you're analyzing the growth of bacteria in a lab experiment. The growth might follow an exponential pattern, where the number of bacteria doubles at regular intervals. By using the **POWER** function, you can easily model this growth.

Here's how:

```
SELECT initial_count * POWER(2, time_periods) AS bacteria_count
FROM lab_results;
```

This query uses the **POWER** function to model bacterial growth over specified time periods, illustrating the function's versatility in various fields.

In data science, machine learning models often rely on polynomial features to improve predictive accuracy. The **POWER** function can generate these features directly within SQL queries, simplifying feature engineering processes.

Practical Applications of Mathematical Functions

Mathematical functions like **ABS**, **ROUND**, and **POWER** can be employed in various real-world scenarios to solve complex problems. In an e-commerce setting, **ABS** might be used to analyze price fluctuations, **ROUND** can refine revenue forecasts, and **POWER** could model the exponential growth of users in a promotional campaign.

For instance, in real estate analytics, investors may calculate the compounded value of their properties over time using the **POWER** function. By forecasting growth based on historical data, they can predict future property values more accurately:

```
SELECT property_id, property_value * POWER(1 + appreciation_rate,
years) AS future_value
FROM properties;
```

This calculation helps investors make informed decisions about potential returns on their real estate investments.

Conclusion

Throughout this chapter, we've explored the vast capabilities of SQL functions in manipulating and analyzing data with precision. From string manipulation to date handling and advanced mathematical computations, SQL functions enable you to streamline workflows and enhance query performance. Mastering these functions empowers you to solve complex business problems efficiently, transforming raw data into actionable insights.

By combining functions like **CONCAT**, **LENGTH**, and **SUBSTR**, you can manipulate text data to suit various reporting needs. Meanwhile, functions like **NOW**, **DATE_ADD**, and **DATEDIFF** allow you to track, project, and compare temporal data seamlessly. Finally, mathematical functions such as **ABS, ROUND**, and **POWER** enable advanced calculations that are crucial for financial forecasts, scientific models, and other quantitative analyses.

The journey through SQL functions is an ongoing one. As your dataset and requirements evolve, so will your reliance on these tools. But with the knowledge gained from this chapter, you'll be equipped to handle even the most complex challenges with confidence. Whether it's cleaning data, calculating time intervals, or performing advanced analytics, SQL functions are your go-to solution for turning raw data into actionable insights.

CHAPTER 8

Conquering the Chaos—Advanced Joins and Set Operations

Well, you've already conquered the basics, but now it's time to embark on an even more thrilling journey. This time, you'll be navigating Advanced Joins and Set Operations—the ultimate test for any SQL sorcerer. Imagine yourself standing in front of ancient scrolls, deciphering runes that will unlock the most powerful techniques for combining and manipulating data. Every spell (or SQL operation) you master will help you reveal hidden insights, forge new paths, and triumph over the chaos of massive datasets.

In this chapter, you'll face trials that require mastery of Cross Joins, UNION and UNION ALL, INTERSECT, and EXCEPT. Your mission is to wield these powers like a master of the arcane arts, conjuring precise results from a maze of tables and data. Get ready to dive deep into SQL magic!

Cross Joins and Cartesian Products

Welcome to the Caves of Cartesian Chaos—a dark and mysterious place where every combination of data is possible. In this realm, you'll learn the magic of Cross Joins to generate all possible pairings between datasets. Your task is to find the right combinations to unlock the treasure hidden deep within these caves.

Mission: The Endless Pairing

In the Caves of Cartesian Chaos, a powerful spell known as Cross Join is cast to combine every row from two datasets, resulting in what is known as a Cartesian Product. Every warrior from the Warriors table will be paired with every dragon from the Dragons table. But beware! While this magic is potent, it can easily spiral out of control, creating more results than your database can handle.

Here's the spell you'll need to conjure every possible combination:

```
SELECT *
FROM Warriors
CROSS JOIN Dragons;
```

When you cast this spell, you'll receive all possible combinations of Warriors and Dragons. If your Warriors table has 10 rows and your Dragons table has 5 rows, you'll end up with 50 rows in total—one for each possible pairing.

But there's a hidden challenge. While cross joins are powerful, they can create enormous datasets, especially when your tables grow larger. If you're not careful, the resulting Cartesian Product could overwhelm your system. Test the spell with smaller datasets first, then scale it up once you're confident in the results.

Bonus Challenge: The Optimized Pairing

The deeper you go into the Caves of Cartesian Chaos, the more dangerous your path becomes. You must now optimize the cross join to avoid overwhelming your resources. Imagine you have two new tables, Wizards and Potions. You're tasked with combining every wizard with every potion, but only if the potion type matches the wizard's magic specialty.

Can you cast a more refined spell using Cross Join and a WHERE clause?

```
SELECT Wizard.name, Potion.type
FROM Wizards
CROSS JOIN Potions
WHERE Wizard.specialty = Potion.type;
```

With this query, you've limited the chaotic combinations to only meaningful ones—pairing wizards with their corresponding potions. You've conquered the chaos and successfully revealed the optimized dataset.

The Duel of UNION vs. UNION ALL

You've reached the Duel of Union Towers—two towering structures where only the bravest SQL adventurers can merge datasets. Your task is to unite data from multiple sources, but which tower will you enter? Will you use UNION, which removes duplicates, or UNION ALL, which preserves every entry, duplicates included?

Mission: Unite the Divided Kingdoms

The kingdom has been divided into two factions—North Fighters and South Fighters. To restore peace, you must unite these warriors under a single banner. Use the power of UNION to combine their names, ensuring that each warrior appears only once:

```
SELECT name FROM NorthFighters
UNION
SELECT name FROM SouthFighters;
```

Congratulations! You've combined both factions into one dataset, eliminating any duplicates in the process. Every warrior now stands united, ready to fight for peace.

Bonus Challenge: Preserve Every Record

But wait! Not every quest demands the removal of duplicates. In some cases, every piece of data is important—duplicates included. Now, you must head to the UNION ALL Tower to combine every warrior's name, even if they appear more than once. Here's how you cast this spell:

```
SELECT name FROM NorthFighters
UNION ALL
SELECT name FROM SouthFighters;
```

In this challenge, you've preserved every warrior's name, keeping even the duplicates. You now have a complete record of both factions—an important strategy when every detail matters.

Strategy Tip: When to Use UNION vs. UNION ALL

Understanding when to use UNION versus UNION ALL is crucial. UNION is best for when you need a clean, unique dataset without duplicates. It's great for generating reports or dashboards where accuracy is paramount. However, UNION ALL is faster and more efficient when you need to preserve every row in your data—ideal for audits, logs, or any situation where duplicates are meaningful.

The Bridge of INTERSECT

Welcome to the Bridge of INTERSECT, where only the strongest and most common data points are allowed to pass. In this challenge, you'll find the common ground between two datasets, using the power of INTERSECT to identify shared values.

Mission: Find the Common Warriors

The North Army and the South Army are fighting a common enemy. Your mission is to find the warriors who have fought for both armies. Use the following spell to identify these warriors:

```
SELECT name FROM NorthArmy
INTERSECT
SELECT name FROM SouthArmy;
```

You've done it! You've revealed the warriors who fought bravely in both armies. These common warriors are now your key allies in the battle ahead.

Bonus Challenge: Discover the Common Treasures

Beyond warriors, there is a hidden treasure that exists in both GoldenChest and SilverChest. Only the rarest coins are found in both. Can you uncover the common treasures?

```
SELECT coin_name FROM GoldenChest
INTERSECT
SELECT coin_name FROM SilverChest;
```

With this spell, you've uncovered the rarest treasures—those that exist in both chests. These coins are now yours to wield as you continue your SQL adventure.

Advanced Challenge: Finding Common Ground Across Multiple Tables

The Bridge of INTERSECT becomes even more powerful when you're comparing multiple datasets. Imagine you're tasked with finding customers who have shopped in all three of the kingdom's shops—MagicShop, Weaponry, and PotionBrews. Here's the spell you'll need:

```
SELECT customer_id FROM MagicShop
INTERSECT
SELECT customer_id FROM Weaponry
INTERSECT
SELECT customer_id FROM PotionBrews;
```

With this query, you've identified the loyal customers who frequent all three shops. These are the most valuable patrons, and you can now reward them for their loyalty.

The Trial of EXCEPT

Now, you stand before the Trial of EXCEPT—a place where only unique data can pass. Here, you'll learn to subtract one dataset from another, revealing only the entries that exist in the first table but not the second.

Mission: Find the Unique Warriors

You've already united the armies, but now you need to identify which North Army warriors have never fought for the South Army. Cast the EXCEPT spell to reveal these unique warriors:

```
SELECT name FROM NorthArmy
EXCEPT
SELECT name FROM SouthArmy;
```

Success! You've discovered the warriors who remain loyal to the North Army. These unique fighters are now your secret weapon in the coming battle.

Bonus Challenge: Reveal the Untouched Lands

The kingdom's mapmakers have charted much of the land but not all. Some territories have only been explored by CartographerA, and it's up to you to find them. Use EXCEPT to identify these untouched lands:

```
SELECT territory FROM CartographerA
EXCEPT
SELECT territory FROM CartographerB;
```

You've uncovered the lands that have yet to be charted by others. The kingdom's expansion can now begin with exploring new frontiers!

Advanced Challenge: Identifying Non-Customers

Imagine you're a shopkeeper trying to discover which of your regular customers haven't shopped at the PotionBrews shop yet. You can use EXCEPT to find the list of potential customers you can target for promotions:

```
SELECT customer_id FROM MagicShop
EXCEPT
SELECT customer_id FROM PotionBrews;
```

With this query, you've identified customers who shop elsewhere but haven't yet explored PotionBrews. Now, you can craft a marketing strategy to entice them to check out your potions.

Boss: The Data Kraken

The wind howls as you cross the threshold into the heart of SQL Kingdom's most dangerous dungeon: the Data Abyss. Here, the Data Kraken, an ancient and powerful creature born from chaotic, overlapping datasets, guards its hoard of precious information. To defeat this beast, you'll need to summon every SQL skill you've learned—Cross Joins, UNIONs, INTERSECT, and EXCEPT—to unravel its tangled data webs.

The Data Kraken is no ordinary foe. It thrives in confusion, feeding off messy datasets that have been joined improperly, flooded with duplicates, and tangled with inconsistencies. You must slay this monster by constructing the ultimate SQL query—a combination of joins, set operations, and filtering techniques—to extract the Kraken's secrets and lay the creature to rest once and for all.

Mission: Untangle the Kraken's Chaos

Before you lies a seemingly impenetrable wall of data—a vast ocean of records representing sales transactions, customer data, and inventory logs from the kingdom's shops. These datasets overlap in some areas but are entirely disconnected in others. The Data Kraken thrives by keeping the kingdom's analysts in confusion, making it impossible to draw meaningful conclusions from the chaos.

Your task is to untangle the Kraken's web by identifying which customers have interacted with MagicShop and Weaponry, made no purchases at PotionBrews, and have never been involved in a special promotion—while still keeping the integrity of the full dataset intact.

Step 1: The Tentacles of Chaos – Cross Joins Everywhere

The Data Kraken begins to thrash its tentacles, attempting to overwhelm you with sheer volume by cross-joining unrelated datasets. Your first job is to make sense of the massive Cartesian Product that it has created.

Begin by filtering the irrelevant combinations:

```sql
SELECT ms.customer_id, ms.purchase_date, ms.item
FROM MagicShop ms
JOIN Weaponry w
ON ms.customer_id = w.customer_id
WHERE ms.purchase_date = w.purchase_date;
```

By using an INNER JOIN, you've started to fight back, narrowing down the dataset to include only those customers who've purchased from both MagicShop and Weaponry on the same day. You've cut off one of the Kraken's many tentacles, but the battle is far from over.

Step 2: The Duplicates Surge – UNION vs. UNION ALL

The Kraken releases a tidal wave of duplicate records in an attempt to overwhelm you. Some customers have been recorded multiple times across different shops, leading to duplicate entries. You must decide whether these duplicates should remain or be removed. The key here is balancing accuracy and performance. To defeat this tentacle, combine the datasets without duplication using UNION:

```
SELECT customer_id FROM MagicShop
UNION
SELECT customer_id FROM Weaponry;
```

By using UNION, you ensure no customer is counted twice—removing duplicates and calming the surge. But the Kraken isn't done. It tries to trick you with some cases where every transaction matters. You quickly pivot and use UNION ALL to include every transaction when the records are important:

```
SELECT customer_id FROM PotionBrews
UNION ALL
SELECT customer_id FROM Promotions;
```

This adds back every transaction, which is crucial when precision is needed. You've now neutralized another of the Kraken's powerful arms!

Step 3: The Grip of Commonality – INTERSECT Challenge

The Data Kraken pulls you into the depths, trapping you with customers who have common attributes across all datasets. To break free from its grip, you must identify the common customers who have shopped at both MagicShop and Weaponry but are entangled in neither PotionBrews nor a special promotion.

Use the INTERSECT operation to find only those who have interacted with both stores:

```
SELECT customer_id FROM MagicShop
INTERSECT
SELECT customer_id FROM Weaponry;
```

With this spell, you've identified loyal customers who are shopping at both stores. But you need to go deeper—some of these customers may still be trapped in the PotionBrews shop. You'll use EXCEPT to subtract those customers from the dataset:

Step 4: The Kraken's Final Weakness—EXCEPT Operation

Now, the Data Kraken is enraged, trying to confuse you with overlapping datasets from PotionBrews. To deal the final blow, you must subtract all customers who have shopped at

PotionBrews from the group that has only visited MagicShop and Weaponry. The EXCEPT spell is your weapon here:

```
SELECT customer_id FROM
(SELECT customer_id FROM MagicShop
INTERSECT
SELECT customer_id FROM Weaponry)
EXCEPT
SELECT customer_id FROM PotionBrews;
```

The EXCEPT operation removes those who have been to PotionBrews, leaving only customers who've frequented MagicShop and Weaponry but not PotionBrews. The Kraken is weakening, and its control over the data is waning as you expose the untouched records.

The Final Blow: Synthesize the Data

The Data Kraken begins to collapse, but you need to deal one final blow. By pulling all the operations together—Cross Joins, UNION, INTERSECT, and EXCEPT—you will reveal the full truth of the Kraken's chaotic data hoard. Cast the following ultimate SQL spell:

```
SELECT customer_id
FROM (SELECT customer_id FROM MagicShop
INTERSECT
SELECT customer_id FROM Weaponry)
EXCEPT
(SELECT customer_id FROM PotionBrews
UNION ALL
SELECT customer_id FROM Promotions);
```

With this final, mighty query, you've revealed the customers who shopped at both MagicShop and Weaponry but never at PotionBrews or through a promotional event. The Kraken's power over your data is shattered!

Victory: The Data Kraken Falls

The Data Kraken lets out a final roar before collapsing into a swirl of clean, organized datasets. You've done it! By mastering Cross Joins, UNION, INTERSECT, and EXCEPT, you've conquered the chaos and restored order to the kingdom's datasets. You now possess the full power of advanced SQL operations, and the kingdom will forever know you as the Master of the Data Abyss.

But remember, adventurer, the real world has many more data creatures lurking in the shadows. Armed with your newfound knowledge, you are ready to face any SQL challenge that comes your way. Let this victory serve as the beginning of many more quests to come!

Quest Complete!

CHAPTER 9

Building Strongholds—Views and Indexes

Welcome back, Database Conqueror! In this chapter, you'll fortify your SQL stronghold by mastering two crucial tools: Views and Indexes. Think of Views as magical windows that allow you to peek into complex data structures without getting lost in the maze. Indexes, on the other hand, are your secret weapon—swiftly guiding your queries to the right data with the precision of a seasoned warrior. Together, they form the pillars of a fortified and efficient database, helping you conquer even the most daunting data challenges. Ready your armor, sharpen your sword, and let's dive into the world of advanced SQL techniques!

Crafting Your Data Fortress—Views

In your quest for data mastery, Views are your most trusted allies. They allow you to transform complex, intricate data into manageable, user-friendly outputs. With Views, you can encapsulate complicated queries, hide unnecessary details, and create a simple way for users to interact with the data. The best part? You don't need to rewrite the same queries over and over again—Views do the heavy lifting for you!

Constructing a View—Simplify Your Data

Imagine you're the overseer of a sprawling city with many districts, each filled with its own unique buildings and streets. If you tried to show a map of the entire city to a visitor, it would be overwhelming. Instead, you create smaller, specific maps focusing only on certain areas, like the marketplace or the residential district. That's what Views do—they give you a clean, simple look at just the information you need.

A View in SQL acts similarly to a virtual table that hides the complexity of your database schema while allowing you to focus on the necessary data. This helps you present only the relevant information in a much more digestible format. Creating a view is easy, and it allows you to encapsulate a query, effectively creating a shortcut for users.

Quest: Create a simple view to show student names and their IDs.

```
CREATE VIEW StudentNames AS
SELECT S_ID, NAME
FROM StudentDetails
ORDER BY NAME;
```

Now, whenever you or any of your allies (other database users) need a list of students, they can simply look through the StudentNames view without needing to navigate the complex, underlying database structure.

Challenge Accepted: Try adding a new field, like the address, to this view. Modify the existing view to include the student's address for an enhanced user experience.

```
CREATE OR REPLACE VIEW StudentNames AS
SELECT S_ID, NAME, ADDRESS
FROM StudentDetails
ORDER BY NAME;
```

Victory! With this updated view, users can now access students' names and addresses without having to sift through a maze of tables. Your city's map has just been upgraded!

The Power to Alter or Destroy Views

Views can grow with your database needs. As your data expands and user requirements change, you'll need to adjust your views to reflect these developments. Thankfully, modifying or deleting views is a breeze.

Updating a view in SQL is as simple as using the CREATE OR REPLACE statement, which allows you to tweak the view's structure without having to delete and recreate it. This flexibility ensures that your views stay relevant as your database evolves.

Quest: Suppose your database has changed, and the address is no longer needed. Modify the view back to just the student names and IDs.

```
CREATE OR REPLACE VIEW StudentNames AS
SELECT S_ID, NAME
FROM StudentDetails
ORDER BY NAME;
```

Deleting a view is even simpler. When a view is no longer needed, you can remove it to keep your database clean and efficient.

Quest: Let's remove the StudentNames view.

```
DROP VIEW StudentNames;
```

And just like that, the view is gone without leaving any scars on your underlying tables. Your stronghold remains as sturdy as ever!

Integrating Views Into SQL Queries

By now, you're probably wondering how to use views in your daily SQL adventures. Well, views are designed to be seamlessly integrated into your queries. Imagine you're working in an academic institution, and you need to calculate the average grade of students for a report, but the student information is scattered across multiple tables. You could create a view that brings together relevant data from both the StudentDetails and StudentGrades tables.

Quest: Create a view that combines student details and grades into one unified table for easier querying.

```
CREATE VIEW StudentGradesView AS
SELECT StudentDetails.NAME, StudentDetails.S_ID, StudentGrades.GRADE
FROM StudentDetails
JOIN StudentGrades ON StudentDetails.S_ID = StudentGrades.S_ID;
```

Now, any time you need to check grades, you can use the StudentGradesView as a table in your queries:

```
SELECT NAME, GRADE FROM StudentGradesView WHERE GRADE > 80;
```

Success! You've just simplified your reporting workflow by integrating a view that pulls data from multiple tables and makes it easily accessible.

Fortifying Your Stronghold—Indexes

Views are your guide through the labyrinth of data, but now it's time to speed things up. Think of Indexes as your turbo boost! An Index can make finding a specific piece of data as fast as flipping through the index of a book. It transforms your database from a slow, lumbering beast into a swift, agile warrior.

Understanding Index Basics

Indexes improve the speed of your queries by making data retrieval faster. When you search through a large table, the system often needs to scan every row, which can be slow. By creating an index, the database can quickly locate the relevant data, bypassing unnecessary information.

Indexes act like signposts or maps that point the way to the data you need, saving your database from performing costly full-table scans.

Quest: Create an index on the S_ID field in the StudentDetails table.

```
CREATE INDEX idx_student_id ON StudentDetails(S_ID);
```

Now, any time you or your allies search by S_ID, the database knows exactly where to look, significantly speeding up the process.

Different Types of Indexes—Choose Your Arsenal

Just as you wouldn't use a single weapon for every battle, there are different types of indexes for different scenarios. Each type has its own strengths, and knowing when to use each one is key to building a formidable database stronghold.

- **Primary indexes**: These are the guardians of your data, enforcing uniqueness and making searches on the primary key lightning-fast.

    - *Use this for your unique identifiers, like employee IDs or product serial numbers.*

- **Unique indexes**: Similar to primary indexes but more flexible, unique indexes ensure no duplicate values are allowed in certain fields.

    - *Perfect for fields like email addresses or social security numbers where you want to enforce uniqueness.*

- **Composite indexes**: These indexes guard multiple columns at once, optimizing searches that involve more than one field.

    - *Ideal when your queries often involve searching by multiple fields, such as a combination of a customer's first and last names.*

Quest: Create a Composite Index to search for students by both name and department.

```
CREATE INDEX idx_name_department ON StudentDetails(NAME, DEPARTMENT);
```

With this composite index, any queries that involve both the **NAME** and **DEPARTMENT** fields will now run much faster!

Striking a Balance—Read vs. Write Performance

While indexes dramatically improve read performance, there's a trade-off you need to consider: every time data is written, updated, or deleted, the indexes also need to be updated. This can slow down write-heavy applications if you're not careful. So, how do you strike the right balance?

For read-heavy applications (where you're frequently querying data), more indexes will help boost performance. However, for write-heavy applications (where data is being inserted or updated frequently), too many indexes can slow things down because the database needs to maintain all of them.

Challenge: You need to decide how many indexes are necessary. Use SQL's EXPLAIN command to analyze which queries are taking the longest time to execute and see if adding an index can help.

```
EXPLAIN SELECT * FROM StudentDetails WHERE NAME = 'Alice';
```

This will show you how the database processes the query, helping you determine if an index on NAME would improve performance.

Advanced Indexing Tactics—Optimizing Your Stronghold

You've mastered the basics of indexing, but now it's time to dive deeper into more advanced techniques. Get ready to wield the full power of SQL's indexing strategies to supercharge your database and leave your competition in the dust!

Partial Indexes—Focusing Your Defense

Sometimes, you don't need an index for the entire table, just for a specific subset of the data. This is where Partial Indexes come into play. They allow you to create an index that only applies to rows that meet certain conditions, making your queries even faster and saving on storage.

Quest: Create a partial index on active students.

```
CREATE INDEX idx_active_students ON StudentDetails(LAST_LOGIN)
WHERE ACTIVE = TRUE;
```

This way, searches for active students will be much faster, and the index won't waste resources on inactive students.

Indexed Computed Columns—Efficiency Meets Power

Did you know you can create indexes on computed columns, too? These indexes are particularly useful when you frequently search based on a calculation, like the total cost of an order or a student's final grade, which combines multiple fields.

Quest: Create a computed column for the total cost of an order and then index it.

```sql
ALTER TABLE Orders ADD total_cost AS (quantity * price) PERSISTED;
CREATE INDEX idx_total_cost ON Orders(total_cost);
```

Now, any searches based on the total_cost will be lightning-fast without recalculating the value each time!

Monitoring and Tuning Your Database Stronghold

The battle never ends! Now that you've built a powerful database fortress with Views and Indexes, your next task is to maintain and monitor your stronghold, ensuring it continues to perform optimally as the kingdom grows.

Monitoring Index Usage

Indexes are powerful, but like any tool, they can become burdensome if not used correctly. Indexes that are rarely used can slow down your system due to the overhead of maintaining them. To keep your fortress running smoothly, you must routinely review your index usage.

Quest: Check for unused indexes and remove them to avoid wasted resources.

```sql
SHOW INDEX FROM StudentDetails;
```

If you find an index that's rarely used, consider removing it to optimize your system.

```sql
DROP INDEX idx_unused ON StudentDetails;
```

Query Optimization—Using the Right Tools

Tools like SQL Server Profiler or MySQL's EXPLAIN command offer detailed insights into query performance, allowing you to pinpoint slow queries and optimize them with better indexing strategies.

Challenge: Analyze a slow query and find out where the bottleneck is. Use the EXPLAIN command and then modify your index strategy to optimize it.

```sql
EXPLAIN SELECT * FROM Orders WHERE total_cost > 1000;
```

If the query is running slowly because it's scanning the entire table, creating an index on total_cost could dramatically improve performance.

Boss: The Fortress Keeper Challenge

As you reach the gates of your SQL fortress, the ultimate challenge awaits—the Fortress Keeper! To defeat this boss, you'll need to apply everything you've learned about Views and Indexes. The Keeper is cunning, and they've set up a complex query puzzle that requires strategic use of both views and indexes to conquer. Only by optimizing both the readability and speed of your queries can you claim victory and solidify your fortress as impenetrable!

Boss Battle Quest: The Ultimate Performance Test

The Keeper presents you with a daunting task: Optimize a complex report query for a global company that needs a quick overview of their sales performance, including the total revenue generated by each salesperson, their department, and the top three products they've sold in the last year. The database contains millions of rows, and without proper indexing and views, this query will run for hours—something you can't afford.

Mission Objectives:

1. **Create a view** to combine data from the Sales, Products, and Employees tables, simplifying the logic.

2. **Add indexes** to boost performance, ensuring that even with large data sets, the query runs quickly.

3. **Analyze query performance** using EXPLAIN, tweaking any inefficient parts of the query for maximum optimization.

Step 1: Create the Ultimate View

First, you need to set up a view that pulls together the necessary data. This view will abstract away the complexity of multiple joins, making the query easier to manage for others in the company.

```
CREATE VIEW SalesPerformanceView AS
SELECT Employees.EMP_ID, Employees.NAME, Employees.DEPARTMENT,
SUM(Sales.TOTAL_REVENUE) AS TotalRevenue, Products.PRODUCT_NAME
FROM Employees
JOIN Sales ON Employees.EMP_ID = Sales.EMP_ID
JOIN Products ON Sales.PRODUCT_ID = Products.PRODUCT_ID
```

```
WHERE Sales.SALE_DATE >= '2023-01-01'
GROUP BY Employees.EMP_ID, Employees.NAME, Employees.DEPARTMENT,
Products.PRODUCT_NAME;
```

With this view, you've organized all the relevant sales data into a manageable format, simplifying the query to focus on revenue per employee.

Step 2: Power Up with Indexes

Now, it's time to speed up the process by adding indexes. You know that queries involving dates and IDs often benefit from indexing, so you'll need to create indexes on SALE_DATE, EMP_ID, and PRODUCT_ID to minimize the time spent scanning the tables.

```
CREATE INDEX idx_sale_date ON Sales(SALE_DATE);
CREATE INDEX idx_employee_id ON Sales(EMP_ID);
CREATE INDEX idx_product_id ON Sales(PRODUCT_ID);
```

These indexes will allow the database to quickly locate sales within the desired timeframe and match employees and products without scanning every single row. The speed boost will be significant!

Step 3: Analyze with EXPLAIN

Now that you've optimized the query using views and indexes, it's time to run EXPLAIN to analyze the query plan and make sure there are no bottlenecks.

```
EXPLAIN SELECT *
FROM SalesPerformanceView
WHERE TotalRevenue > 10000
ORDER BY TotalRevenue DESC
LIMIT 10;
```

Check the output carefully. If you notice any full table scans or performance issues, you may need to tweak your indexing strategy further.

Victory: Conquering the Fortress Keeper!

Congratulations! By combining the power of views and indexes, you've defeated the Fortress Keeper and optimized the query to run efficiently, even with massive datasets. Your SQL fortress is now fortified, and your performance is unmatched. You've proven yourself to be a master of database optimization, ensuring that your stronghold will stand strong against any data challenge.

Bonus Challenge: Can you take it a step further? Add a materialized view to store the results of this frequently-run query, cutting down on repeated calculations. It's a powerful way to reduce load for large databases!

Adventure continues...

CHAPTER 10

Guardians of Data—Transactions and Security

Welcome, adventurer! You have reached a critical stage in your journey through the SQL Kingdom. Ahead lies a crucial task: defending the integrity and security of your data. You are about to become a Data Guardian, sworn to protect the treasure trove of information under your command. But this won't be easy. You'll need to learn powerful techniques to ensure that every transaction is executed perfectly, all while guarding against intrusions and ensuring that your data remains intact through every trial.

Your quest will teach you the use of vital tools like COMMIT and ROLLBACK, the keys to mastering transaction control. You'll also venture into the world of isolation levels, locking mechanisms, and user privileges—essential defenses against errors and data tampering. Can you balance the art of protecting data while allowing it to flourish under your watch?

The Art of COMMIT and ROLLBACK

Mission: You've been appointed as the protector of the royal treasury, where transactions between merchants, bankers, and citizens are processed daily. Every coin, every item of value, must be accounted for with precision. You're responsible for ensuring that all transactions are completed correctly—or undone if things go wrong.

Understanding Transactions

Imagine you're the overseer at a grand market where transactions never stop. You can track every sale, purchase, or exchange, and nothing should be final until you give your approval.

In SQL, a transaction is similar—a group of operations bundled together. Either everything succeeds, or nothing does. This way, you protect your data from incomplete or erroneous changes.

Every time a transaction starts, it's like you're watching a trade happen. But until you approve it, the deal isn't done. Now, the question is, do you COMMIT it, making it official, or do you ROLLBACK, reversing everything if something goes wrong?

Using COMMIT: Claim the Treasure!

You are like the sculptor who won't unveil their masterpiece until the final touch is perfect. Once you're satisfied with how the transaction has played out, it's time to lock it in place with COMMIT. When you issue a COMMIT command, all changes in the transaction are saved forever—just like sealing a royal decree.

Objective: Finalize a sequence of operations that successfully transfer gold between two vaults in the treasury.

```
BEGIN TRANSACTION;
UPDATE vault SET gold_amount = gold_amount - 100 WHERE vault_id = 1;
UPDATE vault SET gold_amount = gold_amount + 100 WHERE vault_id = 2;
COMMIT;
```

When the COMMIT command is issued, the treasury records now reflect the new balances and the gold has been securely moved. There's no going back once you've committed—the transaction is locked into history!

Using ROLLBACK: Undo the Chaos

Even the best-laid plans can go awry. Imagine you've accidentally withdrawn gold from the wrong vault or, worse, charged the wrong account. Disaster looms! But fear not, Guardian, for the ROLLBACK command is your time-travel device. You can undo all the changes since the transaction began as if the mistake never happened.

Objective: Use ROLLBACK to reverse a transaction where funds were incorrectly transferred.

```
BEGIN TRANSACTION;
UPDATE vault SET gold_amount = gold_amount - 100 WHERE vault_id = 1;
UPDATE vault SET gold_amount = gold_amount + 100 WHERE vault_id = 999;
```

```
-- Oops! Wrong vault!
ROLLBACK;
```

With a simple ROLLBACK, the system returns to the state it was in before the error occurred, saving you from catastrophe and ensuring the integrity of your treasury records.

Combining COMMIT and ROLLBACK: Balancing the Scales

Now that you wield the powers of both COMMIT and ROLLBACK, it's time to put them to the test. Imagine you're managing dozens of simultaneous transactions at the grand feast in the kingdom. Every chef, merchant, and trader is moving goods, making exchanges, and balancing accounts. It's your job to ensure that every transaction completes perfectly—or to undo them if something goes wrong.

In SQL, when multiple transactions are processed simultaneously, you must decide when to commit and when to roll back. Think of this as managing an orchestra: each musician (transaction) must play in harmony. If one note is out of tune, you can stop the performance and start over or finish with a perfect crescendo.

Mission Objective: Use COMMIT and ROLLBACK to finalize or undo changes across multiple transactions.

Imagine the following scenario in an online bookstore:

```
BEGIN TRANSACTION;
-- Step 1: Verify inventory
UPDATE books SET stock = stock - 1 WHERE book_id = 10;
-- Step 2: Charge the customer
UPDATE customers SET balance = balance - 25 WHERE customer_id = 123;
-- Step 3: Update sales records
INSERT INTO sales (book_id, customer_id, amount) VALUES (10, 123, 25);

-- If everything goes well, COMMIT!
COMMIT;
```

But if stock is insufficient or the customer's payment fails:

```
-- If there's a problem, undo all changes.
ROLLBACK;
```

Congratulations! You've balanced the scales, and your database remains accurate and consistent thanks to your expert use of COMMIT and ROLLBACK.

The Battle of Concurrent Transactions

Now comes your next challenge: the bustling markets of the SQL Kingdom. Everyone is rushing to trade, buy, and sell at the same time. How can you ensure that no two transactions interfere with one another?

This is where isolation levels come into play. Think of them as the fortifications you place between each transaction, preventing data from leaking across boundaries or being altered midway through a process.

Isolation Levels: Choosing Your Shield

In SQL, isolation levels control how much interaction (or interference) transactions can have with one another. You need to choose the right level of isolation for each situation, balancing performance and data integrity. Here are your choices:

- **Read uncommitted:** A weak shield. Transactions can see each other's uncommitted changes. While fast, this can lead to dirty reads (bad data).

- **Read committed:** A stronger shield. Transactions can only see committed data—no dirty reads, but other issues (like phantom reads) can still happen.

- **Repeatable read:** Even stronger. Once a transaction reads data, no one else can change that data until the transaction finishes.

- **Serializable:** The ultimate defense! Transactions are completely isolated, as if they run one after another in sequence. It's the most secure but also the slowest.

Using Isolation Levels: Preventing Transaction Collisions

You must now control the flow of transactions in the marketplace to prevent chaos. For example, let's say you're overseeing an auction house where multiple buyers are placing bids on rare items. You want to make sure that once a bid is placed, no one can modify the bid data until the auction is over.

Objective: Set the isolation level to Repeatable Read so that bid data cannot be changed once a transaction reads it.

```
SET TRANSACTION ISOLATION LEVEL REPEATABLE READ;
BEGIN TRANSACTION;
SELECT * FROM bids WHERE item_id = 7;
-- This ensures that no one else can modify the bid on this item until
you finish your work!
COMMIT;
```

Success! You've prevented other buyers from changing the bid data mid-transaction, ensuring a fair auction.

Locking Mechanisms: Securing the Gates

The next part of your mission involves locking gates—allowing some transactions to proceed while preventing others. In SQL, locks ensure that transactions can't clash. Some locks allow multiple people to look at data, but no one can modify it (shared locks). Others prevent all access until the transaction is complete (exclusive locks).

Shared Locks: These are ideal for SELECT queries where multiple transactions need to read the same data. Everyone can see the records, but no one can change them while the lock is active.

Exclusive Locks: These are like closing and bolting the gates. Only one transaction can modify the data, and no other transaction can even read it until the lock is released.

Locking Down the Vault: Exclusive Locks in Action

Imagine a royal adviser is updating the treasury records. No one else should be able to touch the data while the update is in progress.

Objective: Use an exclusive lock to prevent other transactions from modifying the treasury data.

```
BEGIN TRANSACTION;
UPDATE treasury SET gold = gold - 100 WHERE vault_id = 1 WITH (XLOCK);
-- No one else can access or modify the treasury until this update is
```

```
complete.
COMMIT;
```

The vault is secure, and the treasury records are safe. With exclusive locks, you've prevented chaos from erupting in the kingdom.

User Privileges—Controlling Access

As the Data Guardian, not everyone should have free access to the kingdom's treasures. Your job now is to manage user privileges, ensuring that only trusted citizens have the keys to sensitive areas of the kingdom.

Granting Privileges: Assigning Roles to Trusted Allies

Imagine you're handing out different sets of keys to your trusted advisers. Some advisers need access to view data, while others need the power to update or even delete records. You must grant privileges wisely.

- **SELECT**: Allows users to view data, like letting them browse the royal library.
- **INSERT**: Allows users to add new data, like adding gold to the vault.
- **UPDATE**: Allows users to modify existing data, like changing treasury records.
- **DELETE**: Allows users to remove data as if they were removing treasures from the vault.

Objective: Grant privileges to the royal accountant so they can update treasury records but not delete them.

```
GRANT SELECT, UPDATE ON treasury TO royal_accountant;
-- The accountant can view and update the treasury, but not delete
anything!
```

The accountant now has the right access to do their job without endangering the kingdom's wealth.

Revoking Privileges: Cutting Off Access

Not all knights and advisers stay loyal forever. If you suspect treason, you must revoke access to ensure the kingdom's secrets remain safe.

Objective: Revoke privileges from a disloyal adviser to protect the royal treasury.

```
REVOKE SELECT, UPDATE ON treasury FROM disloyal_advisor;
-- Access revoked. The treasury is safe once again!
```

You've successfully removed the adviser's access, protecting the kingdom from a potential threat.

Role-Based Access Control (RBAC)—Building a Secure Hierarchy

As the kingdom grows, managing individual privileges becomes a Herculean task. That's where Role-Based Access Control (RBAC) comes in. RBAC allows you to define roles (such as "Treasurer" or "Knight") and assign privileges to these roles. When a citizen is granted a role, they inherit all the associated privileges.

Creating Roles: Empowering the Kingdom

Your next mission is to create roles for key positions in the kingdom and ensure that each role has the appropriate level of access.

Objective: Create roles for the Treasurer and Merchant and assign them the right privileges.

```
CREATE ROLE Treasurer;
GRANT SELECT, UPDATE ON treasury TO Treasurer;

CREATE ROLE Merchant;
GRANT SELECT ON markets TO Merchant;
```

Now, whenever a new Treasurer or Merchant joins the kingdom, they can simply be assigned to the appropriate role, gaining the necessary access without you having to manually adjust their privileges.

Boss Battle: The Final Trial—The Siege of Data Integrity

Welcome to the ultimate showdown, Data Guardian. Your kingdom is under siege! The Chaos Bringer, a malevolent entity seeking to corrupt your data, has launched an all-out assault on your SQL kingdom. He's sending waves of rogue transactions, locking mechanisms, and unauthorized users to breach your defenses. Your mission is to protect the treasure trove of data, keep transactions intact, and prevent the Chaos Bringer from stealing your kingdom's most valuable secrets.

The Chaos Bringer has three powerful stages of attack, each deadlier than the last. To prevail, you must use every tool you've mastered—COMMIT, ROLLBACK, isolation levels, locks, and user privileges—to repel the assault and maintain your kingdom's data integrity. Fail, and the Chaos Bringer will reign over the ruins of your data, leaving your kingdom in disarray.

Stage 1: Transactional Turmoil—The Flood of Uncommitted Changes

The Chaos Bringer starts his attack by flooding your kingdom with rogue transactions. These malicious operations are designed to corrupt your data, leaving behind a trail of incomplete, erroneous updates. The air is thick with uncertainty, and you can sense the danger of partial changes lurking in the shadows.

Your first task is to manage the chaos by carefully deploying COMMIT and ROLLBACK to control the flow of transactions. The rogue transactions must be neutralized before they corrupt the database!

Mission Objective: Neutralize Rogue Transactions

The Chaos Bringer's minions have launched a series of malicious updates across your kingdom's databases. Some of these transactions are designed to corrupt your treasury, while others are tampering with the inventory records. Your job is to ensure that no transaction gets finalized unless it is completely accurate.

- **Solution:** As you review each transaction, carefully choose whether to COMMIT (if the transaction is valid) or ROLLBACK (if any part of it is incorrect). This is your chance to neutralize incomplete or erroneous updates!

```
BEGIN TRANSACTION;
-- Transaction 1: Attempting to update treasury incorrectly
UPDATE treasury SET gold = gold - 500 WHERE vault_id = 3;
-- An error occurs—it's a rogue transaction!
ROLLBACK;


BEGIN TRANSACTION;
-- Transaction 2: Valid update to customer accounts
UPDATE customers SET balance = balance - 50 WHERE customer_id = 123;
-- All steps are valid, so commit the transaction!
COMMIT;
```

You successfully repel the rogue transactions and finalize the legitimate updates. The Chaos Bringer is forced to retreat, but this is only the beginning. He's regrouping for his next assault.

Stage 2: The Lockdown—Breaking Through the Fortified Gates

Angered by his initial failure, the Chaos Bringer sends an even more devious attack. This time, he attempts to manipulate the kingdom's locks, creating deadlocks and halting critical transactions. The gates of your data kingdom are being slammed shut, preventing honest transactions from proceeding. Meanwhile, rogue transactions attempt to force their way through by holding exclusive locks on essential data.

Mission Objective: Defend Against Locking Attacks and Prevent Deadlocks

The Chaos Bringer is using malicious locking strategies to cause deadlocks and prevent your database from functioning smoothly. If too many deadlocks occur, the kingdom will grind to a halt, and you'll lose valuable data.

- **Solution:** Carefully manage locks by using shared and exclusive locking mechanisms. Identify deadlocks and break them before they paralyze the kingdom. Make sure to prioritize essential transactions!

Shared Lock Example: Keep the markets open while preventing anyone from tampering with the records.

```
BEGIN TRANSACTION;
-- Place a shared lock on the marketplace records so others can read
```

```
but not change them
SELECT * FROM marketplace WITH (HOLDLOCK);
```

Exclusive Lock Example: Close off the treasury for essential updates to prevent rogue access.

```
BEGIN TRANSACTION;
-- Apply an exclusive lock to the treasury to update safely
UPDATE treasury SET gold = gold + 300 WHERE vault_id = 2 WITH (XLOCK);
COMMIT;
```

Breaking a Deadlock: One of the Chaos Bringer's minions is caught in a deadlock, holding the vault hostage while another transaction needs access.

```
-- Detect and break the deadlock by aborting one of the conflicting
transactions
ROLLBACK;
-- Allow the legitimate transaction to proceed
COMMIT;
```

You've successfully managed the locking mechanisms, ensuring the kingdom's gates remain secure and transactions can proceed. The Chaos Bringer's tricks have been foiled again!

Stage 3: The Invasion of Intruders—Unauthorized Access

Desperate to break through your defenses, the Chaos Bringer sends an army of rogue users to infiltrate your databases. These intruders are attempting to access sensitive information, including the treasury records and the royal vaults. If they gain access, they'll steal your kingdom's most valuable data.

It's time to stand firm and lock down user access. Only trusted citizens may enter these sacred halls. You must carefully review user privileges, revoke access from those who shouldn't have it, and ensure the kingdom's most sensitive areas are protected.

Mission Objective: Revoke Unauthorized Access and Assign Secure Roles
The Chaos Bringer's rogue agents are trying to access the treasury and customer records without permission. You need to act swiftly to revoke their access and ensure only the right users have privileges to perform critical tasks.

- **Solution**: Assign appropriate roles, revoke privileges from rogue users, and fortify the kingdom's defenses by creating secure roles for trusted citizens.

Revoking Privileges:

A rogue adviser has been caught trying to access the royal vault. Revoke their access immediately!

```
REVOKE ALL PRIVILEGES ON treasury FROM rogue_adviser;
```

Creating Roles for Security:

Create secure roles for your trusted advisers. Only those assigned to the Treasurer role should be able to modify the treasury's records.

```
CREATE ROLE Treasurer;
GRANT SELECT, UPDATE ON treasury TO Treasurer;

-- Assigning the trusted royal accountant to the Treasurer role
GRANT Treasurer TO royal_accountant;
```

Audit Logs:

Use audit logs to monitor activity and catch any remaining intruders trying to access sensitive areas.

```
-- Check the audit logs for any suspicious activity
SELECT * FROM audit_logs WHERE action = 'unauthorized access';
```

You've successfully secured your kingdom's most sensitive data and prevented the Chaos Bringer's intruders from stealing valuable information.

Final Victory: Defeating the Chaos Bringer

The Chaos Bringer has been defeated! You've withstood the flood of rogue transactions, broken through deadlocks, and revoked unauthorized access to your kingdom's most valuable secrets. Your mastery over COMMIT, ROLLBACK, locking mechanisms, and user privileges has secured the SQL Kingdom for generations to come.

As a true Data Guardian, you've proven your skill in balancing power and security. The kingdom is safe, the treasure troves of data are intact, and your reign over the data fortress is unchallenged.

Congratulations, Guardian! The SQL Kingdom is safe under your watchful eye.

CHAPTER 11

The Final Boss Battle: Real-World Scenarios

You've battled through countless SQL challenges—crafted queries, joined tables, created views, optimized indexes, and secured databases. But every adventure leads to the ultimate test: the Final Boss Battle. In this chapter, you'll face real-world SQL scenarios that stretch your skills, combining everything you've learned in this journey to solve business-critical problems. Imagine standing at the edge of a dark, winding tunnel, armed with your SQL sword, ready to face the ultimate adversary: complex data and business challenges that require precision, optimization, and strategy.

Entering the Arena: Identifying Customer Trends—The Crystal Ball Quest

You find yourself in the grand hall of an ancient data castle. Your mission is clear: decipher the past to predict the future. Businesses need insight into their customers, and it's up to you to wield the power of SQL to reveal hidden patterns. The Crystal Ball Quest begins now.

The retail company you're working with has mountains of sales data. They want to understand which products their customers love and, more importantly, when they love them. Your challenge: write an SQL query that identifies the top-selling products across different seasons.

Challenge #1

Using SQL, identify the top five products that customers purchase during the holiday season (November to December).

Hint: Begin by writing a query that counts the number of purchases per product for the holiday season.

```
SELECT product_id, COUNT(*) as purchase_count
FROM sales
WHERE created_date BETWEEN '2024-11-01' AND '2024-12-31'
GROUP BY product_id
ORDER BY purchase_count DESC
LIMIT 5;
```

Boom! You've unlocked the Top Seller Badge. Your SQL skills just helped the company predict which products to stockpile for the upcoming holiday season. With these insights, marketing can also plan better-targeted campaigns, ensuring those top products hit their audience at the right time.

But wait—there's more! The challenge intensifies: can you uncover product patterns for different customer demographics?

Challenge #2

Use SQL to segment customers based on age groups and see if different age groups prefer different products.

```
SELECT product_id, COUNT(*) as purchase_count, age_group
FROM sales
JOIN customers ON sales.customer_id = customers.customer_id
WHERE created_date BETWEEN '2024-11-01' AND '2024-12-31'
GROUP BY product_id, age_group
ORDER BY purchase_count DESC;
```

Now you've unlocked the Customer Trend Master's Medal! The retail team can tailor their marketing campaigns to specific customer age groups based on their product preferences. And with your SQL wizardry, they'll be able to create bundled deals targeting these demographics. You've proven yourself capable of revealing valuable customer insights—something every business needs.

Level Up Opportunity: Take your query a step further by calculating average spending per age group for the holiday season. These additional insights will help refine pricing strategies.

Monitoring Sales Performance—The Scorekeeper's Challenge

You've reached the next level, and here, you'll step into the shoes of the Scorekeeper. The company's management needs a real-time view of its sales performance. They want to know how daily sales are trending and how this year compares to last year. This is a high-stakes challenge requiring precision, accuracy, and—most importantly—speed. SQL will be your tool to monitor the battlefield, ensuring your team has the data it needs to stay ahead of the competition.

Challenge #3

Your task is to write a query that calculates total sales per day for this year. The management team needs a clear view of the highs and lows to make critical decisions on inventory and sales strategy.

```sql
SELECT DATE(created_date) as sales_date, SUM(sales_amount) as total_sales
FROM sales
WHERE created_date BETWEEN '2024-01-01' AND '2024-12-31'
GROUP BY sales_date
ORDER BY sales_date;
```

Success! You've earned the Sales Watcher's Cape. Armed with this query, the sales team can easily track performance, identifying which days bring in the most revenue and where efforts need to be ramped up. Now, they can strategically deploy marketing and promotions, ensuring consistent growth.

But there's a twist—management also wants to know how this year's sales compare to last year's performance.

Challenge #4

Modify your query to calculate sales performance for the same period in the previous year and generate a comparison report.

```
SELECT
    DATE(created_date) as sales_date,
    SUM(sales_amount) as total_sales_2024,
    (SELECT SUM(sales_amount) FROM sales WHERE created_date BETWEEN
'2023-01-01' AND '2023-12-31') as total_sales_2023
FROM sales
WHERE created_date BETWEEN '2024-01-01' AND '2024-12-31'
GROUP BY sales_date
ORDER BY sales_date;
```

You've unlocked the Year-Over-Year Analyst's Sword! With this comparative view, the management team can see how well this year is performing against last year and can make adjustments accordingly. Are sales improving? What products are contributing to the growth? You're helping them spot trends, avoid pitfalls, and make real-time strategic decisions.

Bonus Challenge: Can you further enhance this comparison by calculating the percentage growth or decline between the two years? Doing so will unlock the Percentage Growth Amulet—a powerful tool in your arsenal.

Resource Allocation—Mastering the Art of Efficiency

Your next challenge is critical for the operations team. They need to allocate resources efficiently—whether it's managing inventory levels or adjusting staffing based on real-time sales data. Efficient resource allocation ensures that the company runs smoothly and can meet customer demands without overextending itself.

Challenge #5

Start by writing a query to identify products that are running low and need restocking. You'll help ensure that no product is ever out of stock, preventing potential sales losses.

```sql
SELECT product_id, stock_level
FROM inventory
WHERE stock_level < reorder_threshold;
```

Victory! You've earned the Inventory Guardian's Shield. The operations team can now rest easy, knowing exactly when and what to restock, keeping the supply chain efficient.

But that's not all. This business also needs help with staff allocation. Your mission is to use SQL to determine when the most sales happen so that staffing levels can be adjusted accordingly.

Challenge #6

Write a query that identifies the busiest hours for the business based on sales data.

```sql
SELECT HOUR(created_date) as sales_hour, COUNT(*) as sales_count
FROM sales
GROUP BY sales_hour
ORDER BY sales_count DESC;
```

With this insight, you've unlocked the Operations Strategist's Cloak. Now, the business can allocate more staff during peak hours, improving customer service and maximizing productivity. You've just leveled up your ability to manage both inventory and staffing resources, making you a key player in ensuring operational success.

Bonus Level: Segment this data further by region to ensure each store has the right staffing levels based on local trends. Master this, and you'll unlock the Logistics Master Key—the ultimate badge of efficiency!

Generating Reports—The Scribe's Dilemma

As you move deeper into the SQL labyrinth, you're called upon by different departments to generate specific reports. Each department has unique needs, and you'll have to be quick, resourceful, and adaptable to meet their requirements. Your role as the SQL Scribe will be to produce reports that are accurate, detailed, and easily understandable by stakeholders.

Challenge #7

The sales team is asking for a performance report that shows how much each salesperson has sold over the last year. Your job is to write an SQL query that breaks down total sales by salesperson.

```sql
SELECT salesperson_id, SUM(sales_amount) as total_sales
FROM sales
WHERE created_date BETWEEN '2024-01-01' AND '2024-12-31'
GROUP BY salesperson_id
ORDER BY total_sales DESC;
```

Congratulations! You've earned the Master Scribe's Quill. The sales department can now see which salespeople are performing the best and reward them accordingly. Plus, this report will help identify who may need additional training or support.

The finance department also needs your help. They want a detailed report that shows monthly sales broken down by product categories. Time to put your reporting skills to the test.

Challenge #8

Write a query to generate a report of monthly sales per product category.

```sql
SELECT product_category, DATE_FORMAT(created_date, '%Y-%m') as sales_month, SUM(sales_amount) as total_sales
FROM sales
JOIN products ON sales.product_id = products.product_id
GROUP BY product_category, sales_month
ORDER BY sales_month;
```

You've unlocked the Category Analyst's Torch. With this report, the finance team can see which product categories are thriving and which ones need more attention. They'll be able to make informed budgeting decisions, ensuring the company's resources are focused on high-performing areas.

Bonus Challenge: Can you create a dynamic report where the user can input a date range to generate a custom sales report? Complete this challenge and claim the Dynamic Report Wizard's Ring.

Debugging and Optimizing Queries—The Code Whisperer's Challenge

You're nearing the end of your SQL journey, but before you face the final boss, you must prove your mettle by optimizing and debugging complex SQL queries. Performance is critical, and as the Code Whisperer, you'll need to ensure the company's database runs like a well-oiled machine.

Challenge #9

You've encountered a slow-running query. It's taking forever to complete, and it's causing bottlenecks during peak business hours. Use your SQL debugging skills to identify the problem and improve the query's performance.

Here's the original query:

```sql
SELECT * FROM sales
WHERE customer_id IN (SELECT customer_id FROM customers WHERE
customer_type = 'VIP');
```

Use EXPLAIN to analyze the performance of this query:

```sql
EXPLAIN SELECT * FROM sales WHERE customer_id IN (SELECT customer_id
FROM customers WHERE customer_type = 'VIP');
```

By analyzing the output, you discover that the subquery is causing delays. Rewrite the query using a JOIN for better performance:

```sql
SELECT sales.*
FROM sales
JOIN customers ON sales.customer_id = customers.customer_id
WHERE customers.customer_type = 'VIP';
```

Victory! You've earned the Query Master's Gauntlet. The optimized query now runs much faster, improving the overall performance of the database during peak traffic times. The system is humming, and you've proven yourself a true SQL warrior.

Bonus Challenge: Use indexing to further optimize the query. By indexing the **customer_id** in both the **sales** and **customers** tables, you'll reduce the time it takes to retrieve the data. Successfully doing this will earn you the Database Speedster's Boots, increasing your efficiency in all future SQL battles.

Final Boss Battle: Defeating the Data Demon

You've climbed the SQL mountain, honing your skills and battling through smaller challenges, and now the ultimate test stands before you: The Data Demon. This Final Boss has been tormenting businesses with inefficiencies, mismanaged data, and crippling performance issues. But you, the seasoned SQL warrior, are ready. Armed with your knowledge of SQL, it's time to take on this behemoth and restore order to the database world.

Prepare for the most intense, high-stakes battle yet. This is no ordinary SQL challenge—it's a three-phase, multi-layered boss fight that will require every ounce of your knowledge, creativity, and problem-solving skills. The victory will not come easy, but if you stay sharp, it will be within your grasp.

Phase 1: The Resource Allocation Challenge

The Data Demon begins the battle with chaos—specifically, chaos in resource allocation. Inventory is mismanaged, employees are overworked during busy periods, and products are going out of stock during peak demand. The Data Demon thrives on this disorder, and it's up to you to bring back balance.

Mission:
Optimize the company's resource allocation by using SQL to ensure inventory is efficiently managed, and staffing levels are balanced during peak sales periods.

Challenge #1: Identifying Stock Shortages

The Data Demon has hidden critical inventory levels deep within the company's database. Products are slipping through the cracks, and many are running out of stock without anyone noticing. Your first task is to write an SQL query that detects which products are running low and need to be restocked.

Your Move:

```sql
SELECT product_id, product_name, stock_level
FROM inventory
WHERE stock_level < reorder_threshold
ORDER BY stock_level ASC;
```

Outcome:

You've identified the products on the verge of stockout. Your Inventory Guardian Blade strikes a blow against the Data Demon, restoring order to the company's warehouse. Now, the team can replenish supplies before sales are lost. But you sense that the Demon isn't done just yet.

Challenge #2: Optimizing Staffing Levels During Peak Hours

The Data Demon strikes again—this time by causing staffing inefficiencies. The company is either understaffed during peak hours or overstaffed during slow periods. Your task is to use SQL to analyze sales data and determine the busiest hours so the business can adjust staffing accordingly.

Your Move:

```sql
SELECT HOUR(created_date) as busy_hour, COUNT(*) as sales_count
FROM sales
GROUP BY busy_hour
ORDER BY sales_count DESC;
```

Outcome:

With this query, you've uncovered the peak sales hours. Now, the company can adjust employee schedules to match customer demand, ensuring no one is overworked and customers are properly attended to during busy times. You've unleashed your Staffing Strategist Shield and knocked the Data Demon back, but it's not over yet.

Phase 2: The Performance Optimization Gauntlet

The Data Demon recovers quickly, and now it's using its most insidious weapon—slow, inefficient queries that bog down the database during critical moments. You've entered the Performance Optimization Gauntlet, and it's time to prove your mastery over SQL's power by boosting the system's speed and efficiency.

Mission:

Optimize the most resource-heavy query in the system to eliminate slowdowns and improve performance across the board.

Challenge #3: Improving Query Performance

The company's sales database is growing exponentially, and a particular query is slowing everything down during peak traffic hours. Your challenge is to optimize this query by rewriting it to run more efficiently.

Here's the original query:

```
SELECT * FROM sales
WHERE customer_id IN (SELECT customer_id FROM customers WHERE
customer_type = 'VIP');
```

It's taking far too long to execute due to the subquery. You realize that you can improve this by using a JOIN.

Your Move:

```
SELECT sales.*
FROM sales
JOIN customers ON sales.customer_id = customers.customer_id
WHERE customers.customer_type = 'VIP';
```

Outcome:

Victory! The query is now lightning-fast. You've unleashed your Query Optimizer's Gauntlet, slashing the Demon's ability to slow down the system. You've not only improved the speed of this query, but you've also made the system more scalable for future growth. But the Data Demon won't go down without a final trick up its sleeve.

Challenge #4: Implementing Indexing for Speed Boosts

The Data Demon's final ploy in this phase is to bury critical data under huge tables, making it hard to retrieve relevant information in time. But you've studied SQL deeply, and you know how to unleash the power of indexes to speed up data retrieval.

Your mission is to add an index to the customer and sales tables to speed up future queries involving customer information.

Your Move:

```
CREATE INDEX idx_customer_id ON sales (customer_id);
CREATE INDEX idx_customer_type ON customers (customer_type);
```

Outcome:

You've dealt a devastating blow to the Data Demon by indexing the right columns and improving query speed across the board. The Database Speedster's Boots carry you forward, propelling you into the final phase of the battle.

Phase 3: The Report Generating Showdown

As you advance to the final phase, the Data Demon makes one last stand—this time by flooding the system with reporting requests from stakeholders, each more complex than the last. The Demon feeds on confusion and disorder, and only your skills as an SQL Scribe can bring clarity back to the battlefield.

Mission:

Generate detailed and accurate reports that will provide the business with actionable insights, defeating the Data Demon's chaos.

Challenge #5: Sales Performance by Region

The sales team needs a report that breaks down total sales by region. They want to understand where their products are performing well and where they need to focus more attention. Time is of the essence, and the Data Demon is thriving on the disorganization.

Your Move:

```
SELECT region, SUM(sales_amount) as total_sales
FROM sales
JOIN regions ON sales.region_id = regions.region_id
GROUP BY region
ORDER BY total_sales DESC;
```

Outcome:

You've generated the report quickly, providing the sales team with a clear understanding of their regional performance. With this data in hand, they can now allocate resources and focus on regions that need improvement. You've unleashed the Regional Analyst's Torch, lighting the way forward for the company.

Challenge #6: Custom Report for Stakeholders

The company's executives need a custom report that shows total sales for the past six months, segmented by product category. This report will help them make strategic decisions on product focus for the next quarter. The Data Demon is trying to stall this critical information, but you won't let that happen.

Your Move:

```
SELECT product_category, SUM(sales_amount) as total_sales
FROM sales
JOIN products ON sales.product_id = products.product_id
WHERE created_date BETWEEN '2024-01-01' AND '2024-06-30'
GROUP BY product_category
ORDER BY total_sales DESC;
```

Outcome:

With your SQL skills, you've created a detailed, easy-to-read report that gives the company's executives the data they need to make informed decisions. You've unleashed the Custom Report Master's Cloak, shielding the company from the Data Demon's confusion tactics.

Final Strike: The Data Demon Defeated

With a final wave of your SQL sword, you deliver the finishing blow to the Data Demon. Every report is in order, every query is optimized, and every resource is allocated efficiently. The Demon crumbles, defeated by the power of your SQL knowledge.

You've conquered the Final Boss and earned the title of SQL Grandmaster. Your journey doesn't end here, but you've proven that no data challenge is too great for your skills. The business world is now your playground, and you can wield SQL to solve any problem that comes your way.

Congratulations, warrior—you've won the ultimate victory!

Victory Lap Unlocked: You've earned the SQL Legend's Medallion. Wear it proudly, SQL warrior. You've earned it!

Conclusion

As we draw the curtains on our epic adventure through the realms of SQLia, let's take a moment to reflect on the incredible journey we've undertaken. What began as a spark of curiosity has now evolved into a profound understanding of SQL's hidden treasures. Each chapter of this book was a stepping stone, each challenge a test of our growing prowess. From the humble beginnings of the SELECT command to the complex labyrinth of joins, subqueries, and indexes, you've emerged as a data warrior, equipped with the skills necessary to conquer even the most daunting data challenges.

Think back to the start of this journey when the SELECT command felt like a sword in the hands of a fledgling knight. It was simple yet powerful—a tool for uncovering the secrets hidden in the vast fields of data. But that was only the beginning. The adventure truly took off when we first encountered the WHERE clause, a moment akin to learning how to navigate through a dense forest. With it, we filtered through the noise, pinpointing exactly what we sought and leaving behind the irrelevant.

Then came the aggregate functions, which transformed us from mere wanderers to seasoned warriors. With the power of SUM, AVG, MAX, and COUNT, we were no longer simply sifting through data; we were summarizing and analyzing vast troves of information with the ease and precision of an experienced tactician. Every GROUP BY statement was like a strategic move on a chessboard, helping us aggregate our data in ways that offered profound insights. We became capable not just of querying data but of telling a story with it—identifying trends, drawing conclusions, and making predictions.

Of course, this journey wasn't just a sequence of technical lessons. It was an immersive experience that combined learning with storytelling. Each character interaction, each boss battle, and each challenge wasn't just about mastering SQL syntax; it was about growing as a data professional, learning how to think critically, solve problems, and develop strategies. SQLia wasn't a textbook—it was an adventure, with metaphors and scenarios designed to keep you engaged and eager to learn more. This approach not only made the learning process more enjoyable but also made the lessons stick. Just as a gripping novel keeps its readers invested in every twist and turn, SQLia kept you hooked through challenges that felt like epic encounters rather than mundane tasks.

This gamified, story-driven approach was no accident. It's based on the idea that learning is most effective when it's fun and engaging. Think back to those "aha" moments—when you finally mastered a particularly tricky concept or when you wrote an elegant query that returned exactly what you needed. Those moments were as satisfying as defeating a boss in a video game, and they're far more memorable because they were tied to the narrative of your adventure. Every SQL function, every optimization trick, and every new concept felt like discovering a new power or weapon, allowing you to progress further on your journey.

Through SQLia's structured narrative, you didn't just gain technical skills; you became part of a grander story, turning what could have been dry lessons into delightful discoveries. The journey through SQLia was crafted to mirror the kind of challenges you'd face in the real world. But here, in this fictional setting, you had the freedom to explore, experiment, and grow without the pressure of real-world consequences. This is the essence of effective learning: providing a safe space for you to push boundaries, make mistakes, and ultimately become better at your craft.

The most significant takeaway from this journey isn't just the technical know-how you've acquired. It's the realization that learning SQL—or any skill, for that matter—can be a joyful experience, full of discovery and triumph. Each time you wrote a query that worked, it was a small victory, akin to solving a puzzle in a role-playing game. Each time you optimized a slow-running query, it felt like leveling up your character. And just like in any epic quest, you faced challenges that at first seemed insurmountable, but with persistence, strategy, and the right tools, you overcame them. You've proven that learning SQL doesn't have to be tedious; it can be exhilarating, like an epic quest with triumphs and eureka moments at every turn.

Now that you've braved the trials and emerged victorious, it's time to wield your newfound skills in practical ways. Knowledge is most powerful when applied, and your next challenge is to bring the techniques and strategies you've learned into the real world. Whether you're tasked with solving intricate business problems or fine-tuning existing queries, you now have the confidence and skillset to face these challenges head-on.

Imagine yourself once again navigating SQLia, applying filters with precision, summarizing data effortlessly, and conquering challenges with confidence. Picture every new database query as a new adventure, where you bring together the tools you've gathered to uncover insights, solve problems, and optimize performance. Whether you're dealing with massive datasets or just trying to pull a simple report, you now have the wisdom and experience to tackle it all.

Your mentor's words echo in your mind: "The true test of your skills lies not in knowledge alone, but in how you wield that knowledge in the real world." These words remind you that the journey of learning is ongoing. You've completed this quest, but there are countless more to come. You'll face new challenges in your career—whether it's designing complex databases, optimizing resource-heavy queries, or even managing entire database systems. But you're ready. You have the foundation, the confidence, and the strategies to succeed.

As with any great adventure, the road doesn't end here. The realm of databases is vast, ever-evolving, and teeming with mysteries yet to be uncovered. Consider delving deeper into advanced topics like database design and indexing strategies, or even exploring other database management systems like PostgreSQL, Oracle, or MongoDB. Each new system offers its own unique set of challenges and rewards, further pushing you to expand your horizons and refine your skills.

Think of this book as the opening act to a much grander play. You've laid a strong foundation, but there is always more to learn and more adventures to embark upon. The road ahead is filled with infinite possibilities, unknowns to explore, and new challenges to conquer. Embrace this ongoing journey with the same enthusiasm and curiosity that propelled you through SQLia. The world of SQL is dynamic and constantly evolving. Staying updated with the latest advancements, techniques, and best practices will be crucial in ensuring your continued success.

Seek out resources, join communities, attend workshops, and engage with the ever-growing expanse of knowledge that awaits. Every new piece of information and every challenge you face adds another layer of expertise, making you not just proficient but exceptional. The adventure never truly ends, and that's the beauty of it. There will always be another challenge, another discovery waiting just around the corner.

So, dear adventurer, as you close this book, know that you've only completed one quest among many. Your skills are honed, your spirit is undaunted, and your thirst for knowledge remains unquenched. Keep exploring, keep learning, and most importantly, keep that sense of wonder and excitement alive. SQL is not just a tool; it's a gateway to understanding, analyzing, and transforming the vast worlds of data we encounter every day.

In the universe of data, you are now a skilled navigator, ready to tackle any challenge that comes your way. From identifying business trends to optimizing performance and managing vast resources, the power is in your hands. As you continue on your journey, remember that each new challenge is simply another opportunity to grow. With the tools and wisdom you've gathered from SQLia, there's no limit to what you can achieve.

The next chapter in your journey awaits, and with your newfound SQL mastery, you are ready for anything. So onward, brave soul, to new adventures and greater heights in the ever-fascinating world of SQL! The realm of data is vast, but with you as its guardian, there is nothing that cannot be conquered.

References

Ali, S. (2023, May 3). *SQL case study*. Medium. https://medium.com/@saharmsmt74/sql-case-study-68111256e8f1

Are foreign keys really necessary in a database design? (n.d.). Stack Overflow. https://stackoverflow.com/questions/18717/are-foreign-keys-really-necessary-in-a-database-design

Atlassian. (n.d.). *Visualizing SQL joins*. Atlassian. https://www.atlassian.com/data/sql/sql-join-types-explained-visually

Bhanushali, V (2024, September 9). *Increasing the performance of SQL queries — Part 2: Advanced techniques and real-world applications*. Medium. https://medium.com/@vaideekbhanushali/increasing-the-performance-of-sql-queries-part-2-advanced-techniques-and-real-world-applications-0b9a8a8ae8ce

BI, O. (2024, June 21). SQL filters in 2024: WHERE vs. HAVING vs. QUALIFY explained. *Owox*. https://www.owox.com/blog/articles/bigquery-sql-where-vs-having-vs-qualify/

Case studies and real-world scenarios (n.d.). SQL DBA School. https://sqldbaschool.com/course/sql-server-performance-tuning/lessons/case-studies-and-real-world-scenarios/

Cavanagh, L. (2024). Securing your data: An introduction to data isolation. *Liquid Web Blog*. https://www.liquidweb.com/blog/securing-your-data-via-isolation/

Chu, D. (2024). *Best practices of data filtering using the WHERE clause in SQL*. Secoda. https://www.secoda.co/learn/best-practices-of-data-filtering-using-the-where-clause-in-sql

codezone. (2023, August 7). *Understanding relational databases, primary keys, foreign keys, and optimized table structures for performance*. Medium. https://medium.com/@codezone/understanding-relational-databases-primary-keys-foreign-keys-and-optimized-table-structures-for-466abc5fcd0b

The complete guide to SQL subqueries. (n.d.). Dbvis. https://www.dbvis.com/thetable/the-complete-guide-to-sql-subqueries/

Database locking & database isolation levels. (2020, March 17). *Retool.* https://retool.com/blog/isolation-levels-and-locking-in-relational-databases

Difference between correlated and non-correlated subqueries in SQL. (n.d.). Tutorials Point. https://www.tutorialspoint.com/difference-between-correlated-and-non-collreated-subqueries-in-sql

Dolan, P. (2019, July 8). *Basic database design principles to ensure data integrity and speed.* Medium. https://medium.com/@chinup.peter/basic-database-design-principles-to-ensure-data-integrity-and-speed-78c11ce2f733

Erkec, E. (2019, May 27). *SQL examples for beginners: SQL SELECT statement usage.* SQL Shack. https://www.sqlshack.com/sql-examples-for-beginners-sql-select-statement-usage/

Gavin, J. (2017). *SQL server date and time functions with examples.* MSSQLTips. https://www.mssqltips.com/sqlservertip/5993/sql-server-date-and-time-functions-with-examples/

GeeksforGeeks. (2017, September 22). *SQL | Subquery.* GeeksforGeeks. https://www.geeksforgeeks.org/sql-subquery/

GeeksforGeeks. (2019, January 9). *SQL | Join (Inner, left, right and full joins).* GeeksforGeeks. https://www.geeksforgeeks.org/sql-join-set-1-inner-left-right-and-full-joins/

GeeksforGeeks. (2024, July 30). *MySQL EXCEPT operator.* GeeksforGeeks; GeeksforGeeks. https://www.geeksforgeeks.org/mysql-except-operator/

Gupta, A. (2020, November 2). *SQL aggregate functions: SUM(), COUNT(), AVG(), functions.* Simplilearn. https://www.simplilearn.com/tutorials/sql-tutorial/sql-aggregate-functions

harryovers. (2024). *SQL uses of "less than or equal to" <= vs. "not greater than" !> operators.* Stack Overflow. https://stackoverflow.com/questions/7999435/sql-uses-of-less-than-or-equal-to-vs-not-greater-than-operators

How to optimize SQL queries with multiple joins in oracle. (2023, November 3). Process ST,. https://www.process.st/how-to/optimizing-sql-queries-with-multiple-joins-in-oracle/

The importance of data driven decision making in business. (2024, June 6). *Rib Software.* https://www.rib-software.com/en/blogs/data-driven-decision-making-in-businesses

Join tool. (2024). Alteryx. https://help.alteryx.com/current/en/designer/tools/join/join-tool.html

Kumar, B. (2023, November 10). What is a SQL join? (INNER, LEFT, RIGHT, and FULL Join). *360DigiTMG*. https://360digitmg.com/blog/joins-in-sql

Kumar, S. (2023, July 23). *Mastering SQL: Subqueries and query optimisation*. Medium. https://medium.com/@sumitkum001/mastering-sql-subqueries-and-query-optimisation-2991ce5db7be

Learning JOINs with real world SQL examples. (2017, June 13). *LearnSQL*. https://learnsql.com/blog/learning-sql-joins-using-real-life-situations/

Manzo, M. (2022, November 20). *Data-driven companies: four compelling case studies*. CodeStringers. https://www.codestringers.com/insights/data-driven-companies-four-compelling-case-studies/

Microsoft. (2022). *Database design basics*. Microsoft. https://support.microsoft.com/en-us/office/database-design-basics-eb2159cf-1e30-401a-8084-bd4f9c9ca1f5

Moreno, R. (2024). *Can I alias multiple columns? How?* Stack Overflow. https://stackoverflow.com/questions/11254413/can-i-alias-multiple-columns-how

Moser, S. (2024). *Should I commit or rollback a read transaction?* Stack Overflow. https://stackoverflow.com/questions/309834/should-i-commit-or-rollback-a-read-transaction

Nguyen, A. (2022). *qanhnn12/8-Week-SQL-Challenge: Solutions for #8WeekSQLChallenge using SQL Server*. GitHub. https://github.com/qanhnn12/8-Week-SQL-Challenge

Nguyen, D. (n.d.). *Using the WHERE clause to filter data in SQL*. Public Affairs Data Journalism at Stanford University. http://2015.padjo.org/tutorials/sql-basics/where-clause-as-filter/

Nurazizah, N. (2024, February 19). *Analyzing data E- commerce with SQL (case study)*. Medium. https://medium.com/@nabilanurazizah/analyzing-data-with-sql-ede78da49573

O'Sullivan, T. A., & Jefferson, C. G. (2019, December 12). A review of strategies for enhancing clarity and reader accessibility of qualitative research results. *American Journal of Pharmaceutical Education*. https://doi.org/10.5688/ajpe7124

OptimizDBA Team. (2024, March 3). *Navigating the future: Key SQL business trends and growth opportunities to watch in 2024*. OptimizDBA. https://optimizdba.com/navigating-the-future-key-sql-business-trends-and-growth-opportunities-to-watch-in-2024-2/

Pattinson, T. (2022, November 9). Relational vs non-relational databases. *Plural Sight.* https://www.pluralsight.com/blog/software-development/relational-vs-non-relational-databases

Porter, A. (2023, March 15). Maximizing data security with role-based access control. *BigID.* https://bigid.com/blog/what-is-role-based-access-control-rbac/

Pykes, K. (2024). *Set operators in SQL: A comprehensive guide*. DataCamp. https://www.datacamp.com/tutorial/set-operators-sql-introduction

Relational vs. non-relational databases. (n.d.). MongoDB. https://www.mongodb.com/resources/compare/relational-vs-non-relational-databases

Rodrigues, V. (2024). *Is SQL IN bad for performance?* Stack Overflow. https://stackoverflow.com/questions/1013797/is-sql-in-bad-for-performance

Sam, D. (2022, July 20). *Locking in databases and isolation mechanisms*. Inspiringbrilliance. https://medium.com/inspiredbrilliance/what-are-database-locks-1aff9117c290

Samadov, I. (2024, January 9). *Correlated vs non-correlated subquery*. Medium. https://ismatsamadov.medium.com/correlated-vs-non-correlated-subquery-7f3f79858799

Schwartzberg, J. (2020). *Present your data like a pro*. Harvard Business Review. https://hbr.org/2020/02/present-your-data-like-a-pro

Selvaraj, N. (2022). What is SQL used for? 7 top SQL uses. *DataCamp.* https://www.datacamp.com/blog/what-is-sql-used-for

serg. (2024). *Does the order of fields in a WHERE clause affect performance in MySQL?* Stack Overflow. https://stackoverflow.com/questions/4035760/does-the-order-of-fields-in-a-where-clause-affect-performance-in-mysql

Solomon, A. (2023, July 26). *Comprehensive SQL learning guide: From basics to advance for various career paths.* Medium. https://solomonadekunle63.medium.com/comprehensive-sql-learning-guide-from-basics-to-advance-for-various-career-paths-3a64e8bab360

Southern, B. (2022, February 2). *SQL best practices*. Medium. https://medium.com/@BrandonSouthern/sql-best-practices-e1c61e96ee27

SQL | TRANSACTIONS. (2017, May 12). GeeksforGeeks. https://www.geeksforgeeks.org/sql-transactions/

SQL aliases. (2019). W3schools. https://www.w3schools.com/sql/sql_alias.asp

SQL AND and OR operators. (2016, December 12). GeeksforGeeks. https://www.geeksforgeeks.org/sql-and-and-or-operators/

SQL errors: Five common SQL mistakes. (2016, December 6). *LearnSQL*. https://learnsql.com/blog/five-common-sql-errors/

SQL for data analysis: Unlocking insights from data. (2024, April 1). *Caltech*. https://pg-p.ctme.caltech.edu/blog/data-analytics/sql-for-data-analysis

SQLGate Global. (2018, October 11). *[SQL Basic] How to work with String Functions in SQL*. Medium. https://medium.com/sqlgate/sql-basic-how-to-work-with-string-functions-in-sql-my-sql-concat-length-substr-c38af03c5c32

SQL GROUP by statement. (2019). W3schools. https://www.w3schools.com/sql/sql_groupby.asp

SQL join tutorial with practice exercises. (2022). Datalemur. https://datalemur.com/sql-tutorial/sql-joins-inner-outer-left-right

SQL join vs subquery. (2020, April 30). GeeksforGeeks. https://www.geeksforgeeks.org/sql-join-vs-subquery/

SQL math functions: ABS, CEIL, FLOOR, ROUND examples. (2023). Datalemur. https://datalemur.com/sql-tutorial/sql-tutorial-mathematical-functions

SQL SELECT statement. (2019). W3schools. https://www.w3schools.com/sql/sql_select.asp

SQL UNION vs UNION ALL: Differences you need to know. (2020). *Stratascratch*. https://www.stratascratch.com/blog/sql-union-vs-union-all-differences-you-need-to-know/

String functions in SQL. (n.d.). Coginiti. https://www.coginiti.co/tutorials/intermediate/string-functions-in-sql/

Ten common SQL programming mistakes. (2009, August 20). Simple Talk. https://www.red-gate.com/simple-talk/databases/sql-server/t-sql-programming-sql-server/ten-common-sql-programming-mistakes/

Ten ways databases run your life. (2018, December 31). *Liquid Web*. https://www.liquidweb.com/blog/ten-ways-databases-run-your-life/

Transaction isolation Levels in DBMS. (2017, December 13). GeeksforGeeks. https://www.geeksforgeeks.org/transaction-isolation-levels-dbms/

UnDiUdin. (2024). *Performance of UNION versus UNION ALL in SQL Server*. Stack Overflow. https://stackoverflow.com/questions/3627946/performance-of-union-versus-union-all-in-sql-server

User access controls: 11 best practices for businesses. (n.d.). Pathlock. https://pathlock.com/learn/user-access-controls-11-best-practices-for-businesses/

Vishal. (2024). *Which of the join and subquery queries would be faster and why? When I should prefer one over the other?* Stack Overflow. https://stackoverflow.com/questions/3856164/which-of-the-join-and-subquery-queries-would-be-faster-and-why-when-i-should-pr

WilliamDAssafMSFT. (n.d.). *Subqueries (SQL Server)*. Microsoft. https://learn.microsoft.com/en-us/sql/relational-databases/performance/subqueries?view=sql-server-ver16

Made in the USA
Las Vegas, NV
28 March 2025